AWS Lambda and Step Functions

An introduction to Amazon Web Services Lambda functions
and Step Functions

HL Fourie

Amazon Web Services, the "Powered by Amazon Web Services" logo, and any other AWS Marks are trademarks of Amazon.com, Inc. or its affiliates in the United States and/or other countries.

This book is presented solely as-is and for educational purposes only. All references to Amazon, Amazon Web Services, AWS, Lambda functions, Step functions and other Amazon Web Services, as well as screenshots and code examples are done for purposes of reference and do not imply any trademark or other rights are held by the author of this book.

TABLE OF CONTENTS

TABLE OF FIGURES

1 Introduction

This is an introduction to two of the latest services that have been added to the suite of Amazon Web Services: Lambda functions and Step Functions, which may be used to create serverless cloud-based applications.

The goal of this book is to provide you with a starting point to learning about AWS Lambda functions. There are many AWS documentation guides and API references which offer detailed descriptions of procedures for creating and managing Lambda functions and Step functions. However there is usually far too much information presented to help gain a quick, introductory understanding of these concepts and ideas.

This book serves to explain the key ideas and give you the "big picture" so you can get up to speed at fast as possible before delving into the details of these two services. Also covered are examples of how Lambda functions and Step Functions can be used to create different serverless applications when integrated with other AWS services.

This book is divided into two parts: Lambda functions and Step functions. Lambda Functions is an event-driven compute service where the unit of work is a single function that is executed in the cloud. Step Functions is a complementary service that provides orchestration and state management for Lambda functions. Lambda functions can be used on their own, although the Step function service provides a framework for developing serverless applications that may comprise many Lambda functions.

Each part has sections on the main concepts, configuration, testing and deployment. Many examples are shown to help illustrate how to use Lambda functions and Step functions.

Since this is only an introduction to these AWS services, it does not provide complete details but instead there are many references to AWS documentation, blueprints and other sources of useful information.

1.1 Amazon Web Services

Amazon Web Services, the leader in cloud computing, currently offers a wide variety of cloud services that may be accessed via a set of APIs. These services include the following:

- Compute services such as the Elastic Compute Cloud service (EC2), EC2 Container Service (ECS), Auto-scaling, Lambda functions, Step Functions and Lambda@Edge.

- Database, Storage and Content services such as Simple Storage Service (S3), DynamoDB, Elastic Block Service (EBS), Relational Database Service (RDS), Glacier, an archival storage service, CloudFront and ElastiCache.

- Networking services such as the Virtual Private Cloud (VPC) with its features such as Direct Connect; the Kinesis data streaming service, Route 53 Domain Name Service, Elastic Load Balancer (ELB) and Greengrass.

- Security services such as IAM for identity, authentication and authorization; and Cognito for mobile user authentication and data management.

- Big Data services such as Elastic MapReduce and RedShift.

- Management services such as; Cloud Formation and Elastic Beanstalk to deploy AWS services; CloudWatch to monitor AWS resources; CloudTrail that logs all API invocations; and OpsWorks, a management tool library.

- Application services such as the API Gateway, Simple Notification Service (SNS), Simple Email Service (SES), Simple Queuing Service (SQS), Simple Workflow Service (SWF), CloudSearch, Elastic Transcoder and Alexa Cloud service.

This book focuses on just two of these services. However, Lambda Functions and Step functions are integrated with many of these AWS services and this will be covered throughout the book.

1.2 Serverless Computing

A serverless computing architecture provides an event-driven compute service where individual functions may be executed in the cloud without the need to deploy, provision, and manage the compute resources on which the Lambda functions are executed. The user does not have to manage utilization, scaling and availability of servers as this is all handled by the cloud service provider.

The serverless compute service scales automatically as the load of service requests changes. Fine grained per requests scaling of compute resources is automatically managed, transparent to the user.

Another advantage is the user only pays for the execution time of individual functions and not for the underlying servers themselves.

An additional benefit of serverless computing is that the software developers can focus their energies on their application domain and need not be concerned with the management and operation of the compute infrastructure. This allows for more innovation of their own new products and services and speeds their time to market.

Cloud compute services have evolved from virtual machines to containers, and now Lambda functions represent the third generation, a more granular form of cloud compute services. Lambda functions are the vehicle for serverless, micro-service computing by providing an easy to use and manage compute resource in the cloud.

Although "serverless" is something of a misnomer because Lambda function run on Linux containers on an infrastructure of many servers, the user cannot access or manage these servers. All server management is handled by AWS Cloud Services. The term 'Function as a Service' (FaaS) is actually a better term for describing ephemeral cloud-based functions.

Step Functions provide a useful means to orchestrate and coordination the execution of Lambda functions for serverless applications.

2 Lambda Functions

The Lambda function service is an AWS compute service that allows you to execute your own code functions in the cloud. This differs from the EC2 service where your compute environment consists of entire virtual machine instances. Like other AWS services this is done without the need to provide and manage physical servers on which the Lambda functions execute. Users are only billed for the actual execution time of each Lambda function instance and not for idle time on servers. Another benefit is continuous scaling of function instances to address varying traffic load.

A Lambda function is essentially the execution of a fragment of code in the cloud environment that is triggered by an event received from an event source such as an HTTP request or AWS S3 service. Lambda functions can be integrated with many of the other AWS services. Lambda functions can receive events from various AWS services and also invoke the features offered by other AWS services or external services.

Lambda functions are stateless, meaning that state is not preserved beyond the lifetime of the function's execution. External storage such as S3 or DynamoDB must be used for persistent storage across separate invocations of Lambda functions.

The basic components of this service are the AWS Lambda service which calls the Lambda functions, the event sources that trigger the invocation of the Lambda functions, and other services that called from the Lambda functions.

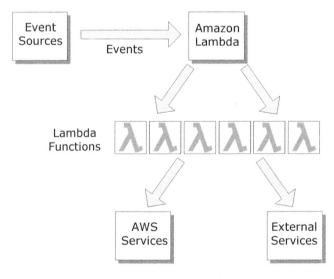

Figure 1: Events and Lambda functions

A Lambda function executes custom code, written in a number of supported languages. The Lambda function infrastructure will automatically scale-out by invoking additional function instances when a function instance is unavailable to process the traffic load. This is done on a per event basis. The arrival of a new event will invoke a new Lambda function instance if other instances of the Lambda function are still processing other events.

Lambda functions also form the Compute services for AWS Greengrass and Lambda@Edge. Greengrass allow Lambda functions to be deployed in IoT devices at the edge of the network. Lambda@Edge is the integration of Lambda functions with CloudFront to offer customized content delivery at the edge of the network.

2.1 The Basics

As an introduction to Lambda functions, this section shows you how to create a simple Lambda function and then invoke it from the CLI. Here is a simple Python Lambda function:

```
def my_handler(event, context):
    return 'Hola mundo!'
```

Store this Lambda function in an S3 bucket. To create a Lambda function, use the CLI create-function command. For example, this command will create a Lambda function called hola with the source code from the S3 bucket using the Python 2.7 runtime environment in the 'us-west-2' region. The handler parameter is the entry point for starting the execution of the Lambda function. It uses the lambda-execution-role permissions.

```
$ aws lambda create-function
    --function-name hola
    --runtime python2.7
    --region us-west-2
    --role lambda-execution-role
    --handler my_handler
    --code S3Bucket=bucket-name,S3Key=zip-file-object-key
```

To get the Lambda function, use the get-function command.

```
$ aws lambda get-function --function-name hola
{
  "Code": {
    "RepositoryType": "S3",
    "Location": location
  },
  "Configuration": {
    "Version": "$LATEST",
    "CodeSha256": code-sha256
```

```
    "FunctionName": "hola",
    "VpcConfig": {
      "SubnetIds": [],
      "SecurityGroupIds": []
    },
    "MemorySize": 128,
    "CodeSize": 265,
    "FunctionArn":
"arn:aws:lambda:region:account:function:function",
    "Handler": "lambda_function.lambda_handler",
    "Role": "arn:aws:iam::account:role/lambda_basic_execution",
    "Timeout": 3,
    "LastModified": "2016-12-22T03:19:03.007+0000",
    "Runtime": "python2.7",
    "Description": ""
  }
}
```

To invoke a Lambda function, use the `invoke` command. The output returned from the Lambda function is saved in `outfile`.

```
$ aws lambda invoke --function-name hola outfile
{
  "StatusCode": 200
}
$ cat outfile
"Hola mundo!"
```

Now modify the Lambda function to take JSON input data:

```
def my_handler(event, context):
    name = event['name']
    return name + ', Hola mundo!'
```

Invoke the Lambda function and supply the JSON input data from a file `input.json` using the `--payload` parameter:

```
$ aws lambda invoke --function-name hola
                    --payload file://input.json
                    outfile
{
  "StatusCode": 200
}
$ cat input.json
{
  "name": "Joe"
}
$ cat outfile
"Joe, Hola mundo!"
```

2.2 Accounts and Regions

All AWS services are created and managed though accounts. When you create an AWS account, it will be assigned a 12-digit AWS account identifier. You can set up the account through the AWS console and then use that account to create Lambda functions and Step Functions.

AWS services are hosted in several locations throughout the world called regions. Each region is a separate geographic area. Some AWS services are only available in some of the regions. AWS uses a set of codes to identify each region.

Code	Region
us-east-1	US East (N. Virginia)
us-east-2	US East (Ohio)
us-west-1	US West (N. California)
us-west-2	US West (Oregon)
ca-central-1	Canada (Central)
eu-west-1	EU (Ireland)
eu-west-2	EU (London)
eu-central-1	EU (Frankfurt)
ap-northeast-1	Asia Pacific (Tokyo)
ap-northeast-2	Asia Pacific (Seoul)
ap-southeast-1	Asia Pacific (Singapore)
ap-southeast-2	Asia Pacific (Sydney)
ap-south-1	Asia Pacific (Mumbai)
sa-east-1	South America (São Paulo)

Use the `describe-regions` CLI command to list the AWS regions.

```
$ aws ec2 describe-regions
{
    "Regions": [
        {
            "Endpoint": "ec2.ap-south-1.amazonaws.com",
            "RegionName": "ap-south-1"
        },
        {
            "Endpoint": "ec2.eu-west-2.amazonaws.com",
            "RegionName": "eu-west-2"
        },
        ...
```

Lambda functions and Step functions are identified by Amazon Resource Names (ARN) which include the region codes and the account identifier. The ARN format and its usage are described in section 4. The account identifier is displayed on the AWS Console Account Settings panel. You can also use this CLI command to get your account identifier.

```
$ aws ec2 describe-security-groups
        --query 'SecurityGroups[0].OwnerId' --output text
```

2.3 Blueprints and Usage Scenarios

The AWS Lambda function console provides a set of blueprints that you can use when creating Lambda functions. These blueprints cover a wide variety of configurations with different AWS services and employ different language runtimes. These are useful for becoming acquainted with the different aspects of Lambda functions and are worth reviewing. Several blueprints are referenced in the following chapters so you can get a quick introduction to the usage of Lambda functions in various scenarios.

These blueprints can be downloaded for evaluation and development.

The AWS Labs GitHub repository (`https://github.com/awslabs`) includes a large number of use cases and reference architectures that use Lambda functions. These can help you in designing your application.

2.4 Invocation Models

There are two invocation models for Lambda functions:

- Push Model. Most AWS services use the push model in which the services publish events to invoke the Lambda functions. This model can use asynchronous or synchronous types of invocation.

- Pull Model. This is only used for AWS stream-based services: DynamoDB and Kinesis. AWS Lambda polls the DynamoDB or Kinesis streams and then invokes the Lambda function synchronously.

2.5 Invocation Types

There are two types of invocation for Lambda functions.

- Synchronous invocation. In this case AWS Lambda returns the output from the Lambda function to the client invoking the Lambda function in a response to the invocation request.

- Asynchronous invocation. In this case no result is returned to the client invoking the Lambda function.

The type of invocation is normally determined by the type of event source. For example, Amazon S3 always invokes a Lambda function asynchronously, whereas stream-based AWS services such as Amazon Kinesis Streams and Amazon DynamoDB Streams; and Amazon Cognito always invoke a Lambda function synchronously.

The type of invocation may be selected for on-demand invocation when the Lambda function is called using the `InvocationType` parameter in the `Invoke` API. By default the synchronous `RequestResponse` invocation type is used, and to specify asynchronous execution set `InvocationType` to `Event`. For a synchronous on-demand invocation, the client will block and wait for the response from the Lambda function.

The input and output of Lambda functions are formatted as JSON structures. A `RequestResponse` invocation type has an input request JSON structure and an output response JSON structure as shown below.

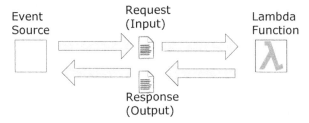

Figure 2: JSON Input and Output for Synchronous Invocation

An `Event` invocation type has only an input JSON structure as shown below.

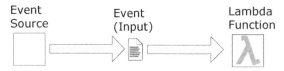

Figure 3: JSON Input Event for Asynchronous Invocation

2.6 Runtime Environments

A Lambda function runs in a Linux container which hosts a language specific execution environment. The language runtimes currently supported by AWS Lambda are Node.js, Java, Python, and C#. Other languages, such as Scala, that execute in a Java Virtual Machine (JVM) can also be used. The entry point of the Lambda function at which execution starts is called a handler.

When a Lambda function is invoked, an event and a context must be provided as the input to the function.

- The Event is used to pass input parameters to the function. An event is formatted using JSON syntax.
- The Context object is used by the AWS Lambda service to pass information about the runtime environment to the function.

When a Lambda function is created the configuration of the execution environment includes:

- Maximum memory size that can be used by the function
- The maximum execution time for the function. After this timeout value the function is terminated.
- The role which specifies what the function can do and what resources it can use.

The programming models for the different runtimes are described in more detail in chapter 17.

2.7 Input and Output JSON Data

All events received and sent by Lambda functions are formatted as JSON. Some event sources, such as S3 or DynamoDB, have well-defined JSON data structures. In other cases the JSON input data depends on the event source invoking the Lambda function.

The processing logic of a Lambda function can access the JSON input data. The access syntax depends on the runtime language. For example, the Python code snippet below shows the usage of fields in the JSON input data structure and the JSON output data in the return statement:

```
def lambda_handler(event, context):
    num1 = event['numbers'][0]
    ...
    return {"sum": sum,
        "zip": 97620,
        "candidate": { "name": "joe"}
    }
```

The Node.js code snippet below shows the usage of fields in the JSON input data structure and the JSON output data in the return statement:

```
exports.handler = (event, context, callback) => {
    var sum = event.value1 + event.value2;
    callback(null, sum);
};
```

2.8 Lambda Function Containers

Lambda functions run a just-in-time environment that uses Linux containers. When AWS Lambda executes a Lambda function, it launches a container as an execution environment for the Lambda function. The container is configured with the runtime and memory resources specified for the Lambda function. The first time a Lambda function is invoked, extra time is required to launch and configure the container. This is called the cold start execution of the Lambda function. Cold start latency can be reduced by using smaller Lambda function zip files and eliminating unused libraries from the runtime image. Cold start latency for Node.js and Python is lower than that of Java and C#.

Once the Lambda function has been executed, AWS Lambda may preserve the container for some time so that it can be re-used for subsequent invocations of the Lambda function. This re-use of the container allows for much shorter invocation latencies and is called a warm start execution.

However, the Lambda function code must not assume that AWS Lambda will reuse the container from one invocation to the next. Instead, AWS Lambda may create a new container instead of reusing the existing container. Therefore, persistent storage such as an S3 object must be used to preserve data used by a Lambda function between successive invocations of the Lambda function.

3 Event Sources

An event source is the AWS service or custom application that generates events that are directed to a Lambda function. Each Lambda function can be associated with multiple AWS event sources. In addition, each event source can be associated with multiple Lambda functions.

There are several different types of event sources:

- AWS event and messaging services such as SNS and SES.
- AWS storage services such as S3, Kinesis, DynamoDB and Cognito.
- AWS endpoint services such as IoT, API Gateway and Alexa.
- AWS configuration repositories such as CloudFormation, CodeCommit and CloudWatch.
- User applications using AWS SDKs.
- Scheduled events. The AWS CloudWatch can be used to configure invocation of Lambda functions are regular intervals.

There are two different forms of data exchange between the event sources and Lambda functions:

1. Stream-based event sources. In this case, AWS Lambda polls the input stream and invokes the Lambda function. Examples of stream-based sources include DynamoDB and Kinesis.

2. Non-stream-based. The event source sends individual events to the Lambda function. Examples of these event sources include S3 and API Gateway.

Each event sent from an event source results in a separate invocation of the Lambda function.

Event sources and their event triggers are listed below.

Service	Triggers
API Gateway	HTTP requests
Simple Storage Service (S3)	Object created events
	Object deleted events
DynamoDB	DynamoDB stream events
Kinesis	Kinesis stream events
Simple Notification Service (SNS)	Messages published to SNS topics
Simple Email Service (SES)	Incoming email messages
Cognito	Sync triggers
CloudFront	Server requests
	Server responses
	Viewer requests
	Viewer responses
CloudFormation	Creation, update, or deletion CloudFormation stacks.
CloudWatch	Scheduled events
CloudTrail	Indirectly via S3 bucket events
CodeCommit	Repository update events
AWS Config	Config rule invocation
AWS Lex	Initialization, validation and fulfilment code hooks
Alexa/Echo	Alexa skills kit invocation
RDS (Aurora)	DB insert triggers

3.1 Event Source Mapping

Event source mappings are used to map event sources to Lambda functions. The event source to Lambda function associations are either configured within AWS Lambda itself or are part of an AWS service that invokes the Lambda function.

In the case of stream-based event sources such as DynamoDB or Kinesis, the event source mapping is configured within AWS Lambda. For example, the Lambda CLI command `create-event-source-mapping` can be used to create an event source mapping from a DynamoDB stream to a Lambda function:

```
aws lambda create-event-source-mapping
        --function-name hello
        --event-source-arn arn:aws:dynamodb:
          region:account:table/table-name/stream/stream-name
        --starting-position LATEST
```

For other event sources, the event source mapping is defined within the AWS service itself. Here is an example of a CLI command that are used to specify event source mappings for the Code Commit event source.

```
aws codecommit put-repository-triggers
        --cli-input-json file:trigger.json
```

Event source mappings will be covered on more detail in the chapter on integration between Lambda functions and AWS services.

For on-demand invocations such as from the CLI or an SDK, the event source mapping does not need to be preconfigured as for AWS services.

3.2 Dead Letter Queues

A Lambda Dead Letter Queue (DLQ) is used to receive information when a Lambda function fails to process an asynchronous event. The Lambda function may be configured with an SQS queue or SNS topic as a Dead Letter Queue destination to send failed requests.

Normally a failed Lambda function that invoked asynchronously will be retried twice, and then the event is discarded. If a Lambda function is configured to have a Dead Letter Queue, the Lambda function service will send unprocessed events to either an SQS queue or SNS topic.

Dead Letter Queues are only supported for asynchronous event invocations and not for DynamoDB, Kinesis stream, or API Gateway event sources.

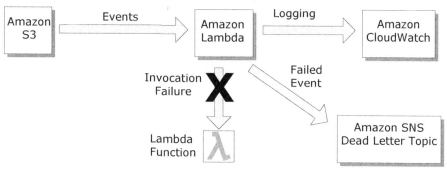

Figure 4: SNS Topic as a Dead Letter Queue

The ARN of a SQS queue or a SNS topic is configured as the DLQ target. The DLQ target may be configured using the Advanced Configuration tab on the Lambda function AWS Management Console.

The DLQ target for a Lambda function may also be configured using the `create-function` CLI command:

```
aws lambda create-function
  --region region
  --function-name lambda-function-arn
  --zip-file fileb://file-path/package.zip
  --role execution-role-arn
  --handler handler
  --dead-letter-config dlq-target-arn
  --runtime runtime
```

3.2.1 Processing Failure Notifications

The payload sent to the DLQ target will be the original event payload. The attributes of the message contain the reason for the processing failure.

When the Lambda service sends an error notification to an SNS topic or SQS queue, it includes a `MessageAttributes` object with the following content:

- `RequestID` – The request ID.
- `ErrorCode` – The HTTP response code that would have been given if the handler was synchronously called.
- `ErrorMessage` – The error response from the Lambda function handler.

For SNS delivery, the `Message` attribute of the `Sns` object contains the body of the failed event. For SQS delivery, the `Body` attribute of the message contains the body of the failed event.

These failed event notifications may then be delivered from SNS or SQS Dead Letter Queue to another Lambda function for further processing.

The Lambda service will increment a CloudWatch metric `DeadLetterErrors` if the event payload consistently fails to reach the DLQ target.

4 ARNs, Versions and Aliases

4.1 Lambda Function ARNs

All AWS resources are identified an Amazon Resource Name (ARN) specified using the format shown below.

```
arn:<partition>:<service>:<region>:<account>:
                          <task-type>:<name>
```

The fields in an ARN include:

- partition is the AWS Step Functions partition to use, usually `aws`.
- service indicates the AWS service used to execute the task, and is either:
  - `lambda` for a Lambda function.
  - `states` for a Step Function Activity.
- region is the region in which the Lambda function is created.
- account is the 12-digit AWS account identifier.
- task-type is the type of task and is one of the following values:
  - `function` – a Lambda function.
  - `activity` – an Activity.
- name is the registered resource name (activity name or Lambda function name).

When a Lambda function is created it is identified by its ARN as shown below.

```
arn:aws:lambda:region:account:function:function
```

There are numerous examples of code snippets throughout this book in which ARNs use *region*, *account* and *function* as placeholders for the actual values.

4.2 Lambda Function Versions

The ARN for a Lambda function may be a qualified ARN or an unqualified ARN. A qualified ARN has a full resource identifier and a version suffix:

```
arn:aws:lambda:region:account:function:function:$LATEST
```

An unqualified ARN only has the full resource identifier:

```
arn:aws:lambda:region:account:function:function
```

When a Lambda function is initially created, there is only one version, the $LATEST version.

4.3 Publishing a Lambda Function Version

When a Lambda function is published a new version is created. When this is done AWS Lambda makes a copy of the $LATEST version of the Lambda function code and its configuration and assigns this copy a new unique version number. The code and configuration of this published version of the Lambda function cannot be changed. The new version has a unique ARN that includes a version number.

```
arn:aws:lambda:region:account:function:function:version
```

For example a qualified ARN for a published Lambda function would be:

```
arn:aws:lambda:region:account:function:helloworld:1
```

The process of publishing several versions of a Lambda function is shown below.

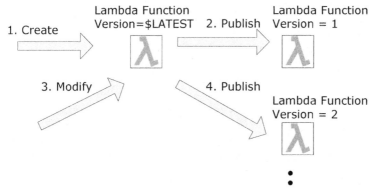

Figure 5: Publishing Lambda function versions

A new version of a Lambda function can be published in the following ways:

1. When the Lambda function is created. The `create-function` CLI command will publish version 1 of the Lambda function if the `publish` parameter is specified.

    ```
    create-function
        --function-name function-name
        --runtime run-time
         --role execution-role-arn
        --handler handler
        --publish
    ```

2. When the Lambda function is updated. The `update-function-code` CLI command will update the code and then publish a new version of the Lambda function if the `publish` parameter is specified.

```
update-function-code
    --function-name function-name
    --zip-file deployment-package-name
    --s3-bucket s3-bucket-arn
    --s3-key s3-bucket-key
    --s3-object-version version
    --publish
```

3. A new version may be published using the lambda `publish-version` CLI command. A new version of the Lambda function code and configuration will be created.

```
publish-version
    --function-name function-name
```

4.4 Aliases

A Lambda function alias is a reference to a specific Lambda function version. It is also a resource like a Lambda function and its own unique ARN. Each alias also has the ARN of the Lambda function that it references. An alias can be updated to reference a different Lambda function version. However, an alias cannot reference another alias.

Aliases can be used to assist with the upgrade and rollback of Lambda function versions. Rather than use a specific Lambda function version directly, it is easier to use the alias and then change the alias as needed for upgrade or rollback to a specific Lambda function version.

This is done by creating two aliases that reference two different Lambda function versions. One alias, for example, PROD, would reference a specific stable, production version of the Lambda function and another alias, DEV, would reference the $LATEST development version. When a new updated version of the Lambda function is published the Lambda function alias PROD can be updated to reference the newly published version.

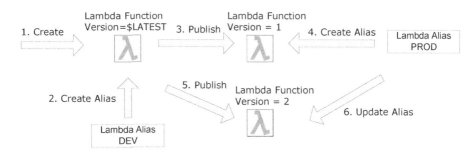

Figure 6: Lambda Function Aliases

Aliases also help with event source mapping. An event source, such as an S3 bucket, should reference a Lambda function indirectly via its PROD alias instead of directly to a specific version. This way the S3 bucket will use the stable version of the Lambda function and the Lambda function association in the event source does not need to be changed when a new version of the Lambda function is developed and published.

4.4.1 Aliases managed from CLI

The create-alias CLI command is used to create an alias to reference a specific version of a Lambda function.

```
create-alias --function-name function-name
             --name alias-name
             --function-version function-version
```

For example:

```
aws lambda create-alias --function-name hello --name DEV
                        --function-version $LATEST
{
  "AliasArn": "arn:aws:lambda:region:account:function:hello:DEV",
  "FunctionVersion": "$LATEST",
  "Name": "DEV",
  "Description": ""
}
```

The update-alias CLI command is used to update an alias to reference another version of a Lambda function.

```
update-alias --function-name function-name
             --name alias-name
             [--function-version function-version]
```

The list-alias CLI command is used to list aliases for a specific Lambda function.

```
aws lambda list-aliases --function-name hello
{
  "Aliases": [
    {
      "AliasArn":
        "arn:aws:lambda:region:account:function:hello:DEV",
      "FunctionVersion": "$LATEST",
      "Name": "DEV",
      "Description": ""
    },
    {
      "AliasArn":
```

```
        "arn:aws:lambda:region:account:function:hello:PROD",
      "FunctionVersion": "1",
      "Name": "PROD",
      "Description": ""
    }
  ]
}
```

4.4.2 Aliases managed from AWS Management Console

An alias can also be created from the AWS Management console by clicking on the Actions button. Select Create Alias from the Lambda function Action menu.

In the popup menu, enter the alias name, description and the version that it references.

Aliases and versions may be listed by clicking on the Qualifiers button as shown below.

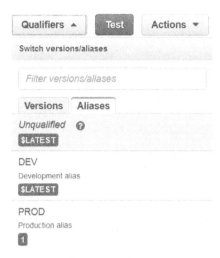

5 Environment Variables

Environment variables can be passed to the runtime environment of a Lambda function. These are key-value pairs that are created and modified in the Lambda function configuration.

Lambda makes these environment variables available to the Lambda function code using standard APIs supported by the language, like `process.env` for Node.js functions.

In addition, these environment variables may be encrypted with a KMS key on the server and then decrypted within the Lambda function on initialization.

Key	Value
LAMBDA_TASK_ROOT	Path to the Lambda function code.
AWS_REGION	AWS region where the Lambda function is executed.
PATH	Contains /usr/local/bin, /usr/bin or /bin for running executables
LD_LIBRARY_PATH	Used to store helper libraries and functions.
NODE_PATH	Used for the Node.js runtime
PYTHON_PATH	Used for the Python runtime

5.1 Configuration

Environment variables for a Lambda function may be configured as follows:

5.1.1 AWS CLI commands

Use the `create-function` and `update-function-configuration` CLI commands with the `--environment` parameter. In the example below, the variable ENV_VAR is set to `Test1`.

```
aws lambda create-function
          --region region
          --function-name lambda-function-arn
          --zip-file fileb://file-path/package.zip
          --role role-arn
          --environment Variables={ENV_VAR=Test1}
          --handler index.handler
          --runtime nodejs4.3
          --profile default
```

The environment variable ENV_VAR is then used in a Node.js Lambda function.

```
exports.handler = function(event, context, callback) {
    var env_var = process.env.ENV_VAR;
    callback(null, env_var);
}
```

This environment variable ENV_VAR may now be changed to `Test2` and this value will be used in subsequent invocations of the Lambda function.

```
aws lambda update-function-configuration
          --invocation-type Event
          --function-name lambda-function-arn
          --region region
          --environment Variables={ENV_VAR=Test2}
          --profile default
```

5.1.2 AWS Lambda Console

Use AWS Lambda Console Code Pane shown below.

5.1.3 AWS SDK

Use the AWS SDK methods `CreateFunction` and `UpdateFunctionConfiguration` and the `Environment` parameter.

6 Security Management

In order to integrate Lambda functions with different event sources, the right security permissions must be granted. If the event source and the Lambda function use the same account credentials then no additional permission is needed for the event source to invoke the Lambda function.

However, if the event source and the Lambda function are owned by different AWS accounts, cross-account permissions must be configured.

Security for AWS services has two aspects: authentication and authorization. AWS services require authentication to determine who may access which service or resource and authorization to determine what operations can be performed for that service or resource. These security services are managed by Identity and Access Management (IAM).

AWS controls access to Lambda functions from other services by means of Roles, and permission Policies. In addition other services must allow access to their services from Lambda functions.

6.1 Authentication (Roles)

Authentication uses IAM users and roles to determine who may access AWS services. Available roles can be displayed using the IAM CLI `list-roles` command.

```
aws iam list-roles
{
  "Roles": [
  {
    "AssumeRolePolicyDocument": {
    "Version": "2012-10-17",
    "Statement": [
      {
        "Action": "sts:AssumeRole",
        "Effect": "Allow",
        "Principal": {
          "Service": "lambda.amazonaws.com"
        }
      }
    ]
  },
  "RoleId": role-id,
  "CreateDate": "2016-11-29T19:53:05Z",
  "RoleName": "lambda_basic_execution",
  "Path": "/",
  "Arn":"arn:aws:iam::account:role/lambda_basic_execution"
},
```

The Lambda function execution role is the role it assumes when it executes. A Lambda function is assigned a role when it is created. For example, this may be done by specifying the role ARN in the `--role` parameter in the `create-function` CLI command.

```
aws lambda create-function
  --region region
  --function-name function-name
  --zip-file fileb://deployment-package.zip
  --role execution-role-arn
  --handler handler
  --runtime runtime
```

AWS Lambda provides a pre-defined Lambda Basic Execution role.

```
--role arn:aws:iam::account:role/lambda_basic_execution
```

Execution roles for Lambda functions may also be created using the Identity and Access Management (IAM) console. Specify the role name, an AWS Service Role type – AWS Lambda, and then attach a policy to the role.

6.2 Authorization (Policies)

All AWS services, including Lambda functions, require credentials to determine whether the access to the Lambda function resource is authorized. In other words, to determine what action a Role or User is allowed to perform on which Lambda function resource. Authorization is managed using policies.

A Policy specifies who can do what action on which resource and when it can be done. These are defined as the Principal (who), Action (what), Resource (which) and Condition (when) in an AWS Policy statement.

AWS provides managed policies that are designed to provide permissions for many common use cases. A managed policy is a standalone policy that has its own ARN and is created and administered by AWS. AWS managed policies make it easier to assign the right permissions to users, groups, and roles than by creating customer managed policies.

Access from the AWS Console requires a username and password. Access from the AWS CLI, AWS SDKs or the API requires access keys.

Lambda function roles are authorized by attaching a policy to its role.

AWS services have two forms of authorization:

- Role-based authorization in which policies are attached to identities such as users or roles.

- Resource-based authorization in which policies are attached to resources such as Lambda functions. These resource policies are called Lambda function policies. Resource policies are useful for enabling cross-account access.

Policies may be listed using the `list-role-policies` and the `get-role-policy` CLI commands. A policy document contains one or more policy statements as shown below.

```
aws iam list-role-policies
    --role-name lambda_basic_execution
{
  "PolicyNames": [
    "oneClick_lambda_basic_execution_account"
  ]
}
aws iam get-role-policy
    --role-name lambda_basic_execution
    --policy-name "oneClick_lambda_basic_execution_account"
{
  "RoleName": "lambda_basic_execution",
  "PolicyDocument": {
    "Version": "2012-10-17",
    "Statement": [
      {
        "Action": [
          "logs:CreateLogGroup",
          "logs:CreateLogStream",
          "logs:PutLogEvents"
        ],
        "Resource": "arn:aws:logs:*:*:*",
        "Effect": "Allow"
      }
    ]
  },
  "PolicyName": "oneClick_lambda_basic_execution_account"
}
```

6.2.1 Managed Policies for Lambda

AWS Lambda provides the following AWS managed (predefined) permissions policies that you can use. These policies include common permissions for specific scenarios:

- `AWSLambdaBasicExecutionRole`. This policy grants permissions only to write logs to CloudWatch.

- `AWSLambdaKinesisExecutionRole`. This policy grants permissions only to process Kinesis streams and write logs to CloudWatch.
- `AWSLambdaDynamoDBExecutionRole`. This policy grants permissions only to process DynamoDB stream events and write logs to CloudWatch.
- `AWSLambdaVPCAccessExecutionRole`. This policy grants permissions only to manage EC2 Elastic Network Interfaces (ENI) for the AWS VPC service and to write logs to CloudWatch.

6.2.2 Permissions to invoke Lambda functions

Lambda function permission policies are used to grant event sources, such as S3, that use the push model the permission to invoke the Lambda function.

The `add-permission` CLI command is used to grant an AWS service principal (who), for example `s3.amazon.com`, permission to perform an `InvokeFunction` action (what) to access a Lambda function (which):

```
aws lambda add-permission
  --function-name function-name
  --region region
  --statement-id unique-statement-id
  --action "lambda:InvokeFunction"
  --principal s3.amazonaws.com
  --source-arn arn:aws:s3:::sourcebucket
  --source-account bucket-owner-account
  --profile adminuser
```

The permissions can be added for the Lambda function version or its alias.

7 Monitoring and Trouble-Shooting

The monitoring and trouble-shooting of Lambda functions can be done using the following features:

- CloudWatch. CloudWatch is an AWS service that provides performance information, logs and metrics for all AWS services including Lambda functions and Step Functions.
- CloudTrail. CloudTrail is an AWS service that logs all AWS API function calls including Lambda function invocations and Step function calls.
- Dead Letter Queues can be used to diagnose failed Lambda function invocations as described previously.

7.1 Logging

If the Lambda function is invoked from the AWS Management console, the following Node.js calls will generate log entries:

- `console.log()`
- `console.error()`
- `console.warn()`
- `console.info()`

An example of a Node.js Lambda function that uses `console.log` is shown below.

```
exports.myHandler = function(event, context, callback) {
  console.log("value1 = " + event.key1);
  console.log("value2 = " + event.key2);
  console.log('Received event:' JSON.stringify(event, null, 2));
  callback(null, "some success message");
}
```

7.1.1 Accessing CloudWatch Logs

The AWS Lambda function console provides a summary of its execution metrics, and CloudWatch can be used to view the detailed logs and metrics generated by a Lambda function. This is covered in more detail in section 12.3.

7.1.2 CloudWatch Metrics

The following Lambda functions metrics are available in CloudWatch:

1. Duration. This is the execution duration in milliseconds rounded up to the nearest 100ms.

2. Errors. This is a count of execution errors detected. This includes:
   - Handled exceptions. Those generated by Lambda functions.
   - Unhandled exceptions. Those generated by the AWS Lambda service:
     - Out of memory exceptions.
     - Timeouts
     - Permissions errors

   An execution error rate should be computed as the ratio of errors to invocations.

3. Invocations. This is a count of all function invocations, both successful and failed invocations, but does not include throttled attempts. This determines the billing charges that are applied to a Lambda function. Memory allocated for a Lambda function is factored into the function billing.

4. Throttles. This is the number of invocation attempts that were throttled due to invocation rates exceeding the limit of concurrent executions.

Alarms should be set up for these metrics to ensure these metrics are reported when alarm thresholds are exceeded.

7.1.3 CloudTrail Logs

A trail can be created from the AWS CloudTrail management console to record API invocation activity for your account as shown below. An S3 bucket can be created to which the CloudTrail logs are stored. When CloudTrail logging is enabled, API calls made to Lambda functions are tracked in log files.

Create Trail

Trail name*	LambdaTrail
Apply trail to all regions	◉ Yes ○ No **ⓘ**
Create a new S3 bucket	◉ Yes ○ No
S3 bucket*	LambdaTrailS3Bucket **ⓘ**
Log file prefix	**ⓘ**
	Location /
Encrypt log files	○ Yes ◉ No **ⓘ**
Enable log file validation	◉ Yes ○ No **ⓘ**
Send SNS notification for every log file delivery	○ Yes ◉ No **ⓘ**

* Required field

Additional charges may apply **ⓘ**

[Create]

CloudTrail trails can be listed using the CLI command `describe-trails`:

```
aws cloudtrail describe-trails
{
  "trailList": [
    {
```

```
    "IncludeGlobalServiceEvents": true,
    "Name": "MyTrail",
    "TrailARN": "arn:aws:cloudtrail:region:account:
                                        trail/MyTrail",
    "LogFileValidationEnabled": true,
    "IsMultiRegionTrail": true,
    "HasCustomEventSelectors": false,
    "S3BucketName": "LambdaS3TrailBucket",
    "HomeRegion": region
    }
  ]
}
```

The CloudTrail logs stored in the S3 bucket can be viewed from the S3 Console. Click on the name of the S3 bucket that contains the CloudTrail logs, and then continue to click through the object hierarchy until you get to the log file that has the CloudTrail log as shown below.

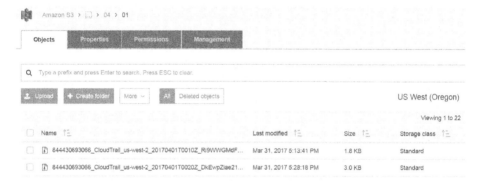

7.2 Common Trouble-shooting Problems

Common trouble-shooting problem are related to permissions.

1. No CloudWatch log records event though Lambda functions and Step Fucntions are working correctly. The cause is usually missing CloudWatch permissions for the Lambda execution role.

2. If Lambda functions or Step Functions are not being executed, ensure that the execution role has the correct permissions to execute.

3. If a "Task timed out after X seconds" message occurs even though a Lambda function has no long duration processing. This may happen if the Lambda function does not have permission to execute an S3 GetObject operation. In this case the Lambda function may continually query the S3 bucket.

7.3 Pricing Charges

Lambda functions are charged as follows:

- Per invocation request. The first 1 million requests per month are free, after which the charge is $0.20 per 1 million requests.

- Duration of memory allocation. The duration is the amount of time the function executes rounded up to the nearest 100 milliseconds. The charge is $0.00001667 for every GB-second allocated.

The Lambda free tier includes 1M free requests per month and 400,000 GB-seconds of compute time per month. There are additional charges if the Lambda function uses other AWS services.

8 Lambda Function Integrations

This chapter deals with how Lambda functions are integrated with different event sources including various AWS services.

In order to integrate Lambda functions with different event sources, the right security permissions must be granted. If the event source and the Lambda function are owned by the same account credentials the no additional permission is needed for the event source to invoke the Lambda function.

However, if the event source and the Lambda function are owned by different AWS account, cross-account permissions must be configured. More details are provided in the chapter on Security Controls for Lambda functions.

8.1 S3

Amazon Simple Storage Service (Amazon S3) is cloud-based object storage service. In the S3 service, buckets are created into which objects can be stored. All S3 objects stored in S3 buckets are identified by a unique URL having the format:

```
http://s3.amazonaws.com/bucket/key
```

Amazon S3 can be configured to publish events to AWS Lambda, invoke the Lambda function and pass the event data as a parameter. Events are generated from S3 when objects are created or deleted in a S3 bucket. Amazon S3 provides the bucket notification configuration API to configure an event source mapping to associate the bucket events to publish and the Lambda function to invoke.

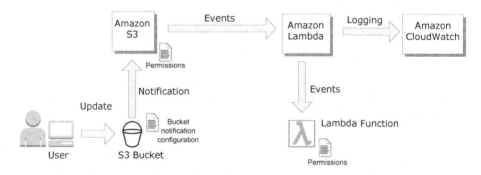

Figure 7: Lambda functions triggered from S3 Buckets

8.1.1 Input Data Format

Each notification is delivered as a JSON object with the following fields:

- Region
- Timestamp
- Event Type
- Request Actor Principal ID
- Source IP of the request
- Request ID
- Host ID
- Notification Configuration Destination ID
- Bucket Name
- Bucket ARN
- Bucket Owner Principal ID
- Object Key
- Object Size
- Object ETag
- Object Version ID (if versioning is enabled on the bucket)

S3 sends events to a Lambda function with a JSON message structure shown below:

```
{
  "Records":[{
    "eventVersion":"2.0",
    "eventSource":"aws:s3",
    "awsRegion": region
    "eventTime":"1970-01-01T00:00:00.000Z",
    "eventName":"ObjectCreated:Put",
    "userIdentity":{
      "principalId": principal-id
    },
    "requestParameters":{
      "sourceIPAddress": source-ip-address
    },
    "responseElements":{
      "x-amz-request-id": amazon-s3-generated-request-id,
      "x-amz-id 2": amazon-s3-host-that-processed-request
    },
    "s3":{
      "s3SchemaVersion":"1.0",
      "configurationId":"testConfigRule",
      "bucket":{
        "arn": bucket-arn,
        "name": bucket-name
      },
      "object":{
        "sequencer": event-sequence-number,
        "key": object-key,
        "size": object-size
      },
    }]
}
```

The contents of the JSON input data structure can be accessed within the Lambda function as shown in this Python code snippet that retrieves records in the array of Records:

```
def lambda_handler(event, context):
    for record in event['Records']:
        if 'aws:s3' == record['eventSource']:
            bucket = record['s3']['bucket']['name']
        ...
```

8.1.2 Bucket Notification Configuration

On the AWS Management console, select the S3 bucket to be used as the event source, click on the Properties tab and then click on the Events tab as shown below. Enter the notification name, the S3 event type and the Lambda function name, then click on Save.

▾ Events

Event Notifications enable you to send alerts or trigger workflows. Notifications can be sent via Amazon Simple Notification Service (SNS) or Amazon Simple Queue Service (SQS) or to a Lambda function (depending on the bucket location).

Name	Event(s)	Filter	Type	
CreateNotification	ObjectCreated (All)		Lambda	✎ ✖

Name	DeleteNotification	ℹ
Events	ObjectRemoved (All) ✖	ℹ
Prefix	e.g. images/	ℹ
Suffix	e.g. jpg	ℹ
Send To	○ SNS topic ○ SQS queue ◉ Lambda function	ℹ
Lambda function	s3-alarm ▾	

The AWS S3-API CLI command `put-bucket-notification-configuration` may also be used to configure a notification for an S3 bucket.

```
aws s3api put-bucket-notification-configuration
    --region region
    --bucket s3-bucket-name
    --notification-configuration file://notification.json
```

The notification configuration file contains:

```
{
  "LambdaFunctionConfigurations": [
  {
    "LambdaFunctionArn":
      "arn:aws:lambda:region:account:function:function",
    "Id": "PutNotification",
    "Events": [
      "s3:ObjectCreated:Put"
    ]
  }]
}
```

The AWS S3-API CLI command `get-bucket-notification-configuration` can be used to retrieve configured notifications:

```
aws s3api get-bucket-notification-configuration --bucket bucket1
```

8.1.3 S3 Blueprints

The following blueprints integrate S3 with Lambda functions:

- s3-get-object. Retrieves metadata for an S3 object that has been updated, implemented in Node.js.
- s3-get-object-python. Retrieves metadata for an S3 object that has been updated, implemented in Python.

8.2 CloudTrail

AWS CloudTrail records all AWS API calls and related access events for an AWS account. These events are recorded in an S3 bucket that is specified when CloudWatch is enabled. The S3 bucket notification feature can be configured to invoke a Lambda function whenever the S3 bucket is updated by a CloudTrail log. The CloudTrail log object is passed as a parameter to the Lambda function.

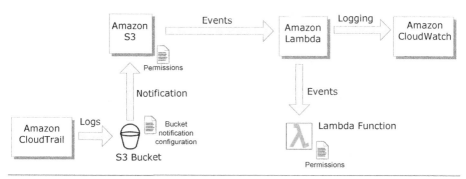

Figure 8: Lambda functions triggered from CloudTrail via S3

8.3 DynamoDB

Amazon DynamoDB (DDB) is a key-value database service that lets you create tables and store information into these tables as key-value pairs. DynamoDB can also generate a stream of events that represent changes to any items in the database. A DynamoDB stream is an ordered sequence of any changes to items in the database tables. A DDB stream is enabled when a table is created. The stream view type specifies what type of information for the item is written to the stream: key-only, the entire item after the change, the entire item before the change, or the item information before and after the change. A DDB stream may be enabled using the update-table command.

```
aws dynamodb update-table --table-name table1
     --stream-specification
StreamEnabled=true,StreamViewType=NEW_IMAGE
{
    "TableDescription": {
        "TableArn":
"arn:aws:dynamodb:region:account:table/table1",
        "AttributeDefinitions": [
            {
                "AttributeName": "tableID",
                "AttributeType": "S"
            }
        ],
        "ProvisionedThroughput": {
            "NumberOfDecreasesToday": 0,
            "WriteCapacityUnits": 2,
            "ReadCapacityUnits": 2,
            "LastDecreaseDateTime": 1480634571.527
        },
        "TableSizeBytes": 91,
        "TableName": "table1",
        "TableStatus": "UPDATING",
        "StreamSpecification": {
            "StreamViewType": "NEW_IMAGE",
            "StreamEnabled": true
        },
        "LatestStreamLabel": "2017-01-05T22:43:50.992",
        "KeySchema": [
            {
                "KeyType": "HASH",
                "AttributeName": "tableID"
            }
        ],
        "ItemCount": 3,
        "CreationDateTime": 1480634524.891,
        "LatestStreamArn": "arn:aws:dynamodb:region:
            account:table/table1/stream/2017-01-05T22:43:50.992"
```

```
    }
}
```

Amazon Lambda may be configured to poll the DynamoDB stream and then invoke the Lambda function. An event source mapping must be configured to associate the DynamoDB stream with a Lambda function. Any record added to the stream will result in AWS Lambda invoking the Lambda function. A DynamoDB stream can be associated with multiple Lambda functions, and a Lambda function can be associated with multiple streams.

For cross-account access, two sets of permissions required:

1. IAM Execution Role for the Lambda function itself
2. DynamoDB permission to invoke the Lambda function

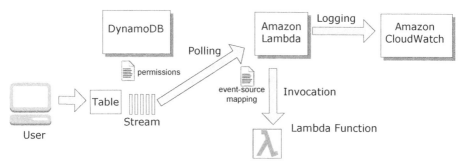

Figure 9: Lambda functions triggered from DynamoDB Streams

8.3.1 Input Data Format

DynamoDB sends events to a Lambda function with a JSON message structure shown below:

```
{
  "Records": [{
    "eventID": "1",
    "eventVersion": "1.0",
    "dynamodb": {
      "Keys": {
        "Id": {
          "N": "101"
        }
      },
      "NewImage": {
        "Message": {
          "S": "New item"
        },
        "Id": {
          "N": "101"
        }
```

```
    },
    "StreamViewType": "NEW_AND_OLD_IMAGES",
    "SequenceNumber": "111",
    "SizeBytes": 26
    },
    "awsRegion": region,
    "eventName": "INSERT",
    "eventSourceARN": event-source-arn,
    "eventSource": "aws:dynamodb"
  }]
}
```

8.3.2 Event Source Mapping Configuration

The Lambda service can be configured to poll a DynamoDB stream and invoke a Lambda function. This is done using the CLI command `create-event-source-mapping`.

```
aws lambda create-event-source-mapping
  --region region
  --function-name lambda-function-name
  --event-source-arn dynamodb-stream-arn
  --batch-size batch-size
```

The event source mapping consists of the name of the Lambda function and the ARN of the associated DDB stream. The event source mapping may also specify the maximum number of records (`batch-size`) the Lambda function is to receive per invocation.

8.3.3 DynamoDB Blueprints

The following blueprints provide guidance to integrate DynamoDB with Lambda functions:

- dynamodb-process-stream. Process a DynamoDB stream3, implemented in Node.js.
- dynamodb-process-stream-python. Process a DynamoDB stream3, implemented in Python.

8.4 Kinesis Streams

Kinesis is a data streaming service. Amazon Lambda is configured to poll the Amazon Kinesis data stream and generate events for Lambda functions.

If the Kinesis source and the Lambda functions are owned by different accounts (cross-account access), then two sets of permissions are required:

1. IAM Execution Role for the Lambda function itself

2. Kinesis permission to invoke the Lambda function

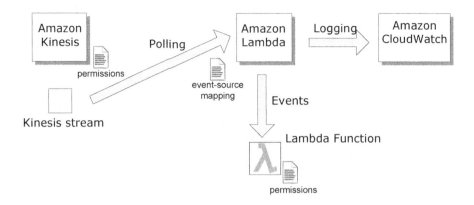

Figure 10: Lambda functions triggered from Kinesis Streams

8.4.1 Input Data Format

Kinesis sends events to a Lambda function with a JSON message structure shown below:

```
{
  "Records": [{
    "eventID":"shardId-000000000000:XXXX ",
    "eventVersion": "1.0",
    "kinesis": {
      "partitionKey": "partitionKey-3",
      "data": "YYYY",
      "kinesisSchemaVersion": "1.0",
      "sequenceNumber": sequence-number
    },
    "invokeIdentityArn": identity-arn,
    "eventName": "aws:kinesis:record",
    "eventSourceARN": event-source-arn,
    "eventSource": "aws:kinesis",
    "awsRegion": region
  }]
}
```

8.4.2 Event Source Mapping Configuration

The Lambda service can be configured to poll a Kinesis stream to invoke a Lambda function. This is done using the CLI command `create-event-source-mapping`.

```
aws lambda create-event-source-mapping
  --region region
  --function-name lambda-function-name
  --event-source-arn kinesis-stream-arn
  --batch-size batch-size
```

The event source mapping consists of the name of the Lambda function and the ARN of the associated Kinesis stream. The event source mapping may also specify the maximum number of records (`batch-size`) the Lambda function is to receive per invocation.

8.4.3 Kinesis Blueprints

There are several blueprints for the integration of Kinesis with Lambda functions:

- kinesis-process-record-python. Process a Kinesis stream, implemented in Python.
- kinesis-process-record. Process a Kinesis stream, implemented in Node.js.

8.5 Simple Notification Service

SNS is the AWS messaging service that uses topics as rendezvous points between producers that publish messages to topics, and consumers that subscribe to receive notifications of those messages.

Messages are published to SNS topics. Lambda functions can subscribe to receive those message events from the SNS topics. The message is passed to the Lambda function as a parameter of the event. For cross-account access, an IAM Execution Role is required as well as permisson for the SNS topic to invoke the Lambda function.

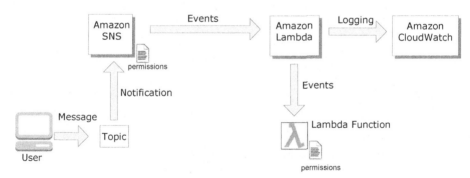

Figure 11: Lambda functions triggered from SNS Topics

8.5.1 Input Data Format

SNS sends events to a Lambda function with a JSON message structure shown below:

```
{
    "Records": [
    {
```

```
  "EventVersion": "1.0",
  "EventSubscriptionArn": event-subscription-arn,
  "EventSource": "aws:sns",
  "Sns": {
    "SignatureVersion": "1",
    "Timestamp": "1970-01-01T00:00:00.000Z",
    "Signature": "EXAMPLE",
    "SigningCertUrl": "EXAMPLE",
    "MessageId": "XXXX",
      "Message": "SNS hello",
      "MessageAttributes": {
        "Test": {
          "Type": "String",
          "Value": "TestString"
      },
    },
    "Type": "Notification",
    "UnsubscribeUrl": "EXAMPLE",
    "TopicArn": topic-arn,
    "Subject": "TestInvoke"
  }
]
}
```

8.5.2 Trigger Configuration

An SNS topic can be configured to subscribe a Lambda function to receive events from the topic using the AWS Management Console or by using the SNS `subscribe` CLI command. In this CLI command the `protocol` is specified as `lambda`, and the `notification-endpoint` is the ARN of the Lambda function.

```
aws sns subscribe
        --topic-arn sns-topic-arn
        --protocol lambda
        --notification-endpoint
            arn:aws:lambda:region:account:
                              function:lambda-function
```

To test the configuration, publish messages to the SNS topic using the SNS `publish` CLI command.

```
aws sns publish
        --topic-arn sns-topic-arn
        --message file://message.txt
        --subject Test
```

8.5.3 SNS Blueprints

These blueprints describe the integration of SNS with Lambda functions:

- sns-message. Logs messages pushed to an SNS topic, implemented in Node.js.

- sns-message-python. Logs messages pushed to an SNS topic, implemented in Python.

8.6 Simple Email Service

When the SES receives an email messages, it may be configured to send events to Lambda functions. The email message content is passed to the Lambda function as a parameter. A list of recipients is configured on the SES service and will receive email messages. Receipt rules are configured for the set of recipients so that the SES service invokes a Lambda function when these recipients receive email.

For cross-account access, an IAM Execution Role is required as well as permisson for the SES to invoke the Lambda function.

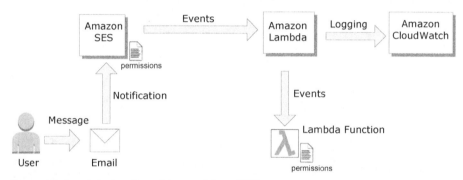

Figure 12: Lambda functions triggered from SES

If the SES service does a synchronous invocation (RequestResponse) of the Lambda function it is possible for the Lambda function to control the SES service by sending certain responses back to the SES service. These response values include:

- STOP_RULE - No further actions in the current receipt rule will be processed, but further receipt rules can be processed.
- STOP_RULE_SET - No further actions or receipt rules will be processed.
- CONTINUE or any other invalid value - This means that further actions and receipt rules can be processed.

8.6.1 Input Data Format

SES sends events to a Lambda function with a JSON message structure shown below:

```
{
  "Records": [
  {
```

```
    "eventSource": "aws:ses",
    "eventVersion": "1.0",
    "ses": {
      "receipt": {
        receipt-contents
      },
      "mail": {
        email-contents
      }
    }
  }]
}
```

8.6.2 Trigger Configuration

An SES receipt rule can be configured to deliver email events to a Lambda function using the CLI `create-receipt-rule` command. A receipt rule consists of a list of recipients that the rule applies to and a set of actions to be performed when an email message is received. One of the possible actions is to invoke a Lambda function.

```
aws ses create-receipt-rule
        --rule-set-name receipt-rule-set-name
        --rule receipt-rule-definition-file
```

The SES receipt rule which includes a `LambdaAction` is shown below in the JSON formatted file:

```
{
  "Name": receipt-rule-name,
  "Enabled": true|false,
  "TlsPolicy": "Require"|"Optional",
  "Recipients": ses-recipient-list,
  "Actions": [
  {
    "LambdaAction": {
      "TopicArn": topic-arn,
      "FunctionArn": function-arn,
      "InvocationType": "Event"|"RequestResponse"
    },
  }]
}
```

8.6.3 SES Blueprints

These blueprints describe integration of SES with Lambda functions:

- ses-notification-nodejs. SES notification handler.implemented in Node.js.
- ses-notification-python. SES notification handler.implemented in Python.

8.7 API Gateway

API Gateway is an AWS service that provides a secure, scalable RESTful API that can be accessed using HTTP requests. The HTTP endpoints of API Gateway are associated with registered domain names. The integration of API Gateway and Lambda functions can be used to create a wide variety of Web applications. Lambda functions can be invoked when the API Gateway service receives various different HTTP requests operations such as GET or POST methods to a registered URI for a HTTP endpoint.

For cross-account access, an IAM Execution Role is required as well as permisson for the API Gateway to invoke the Lambda function.

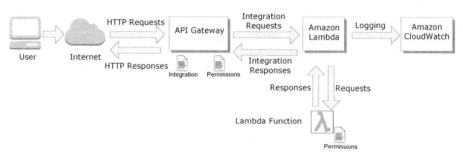

Figure 13: Lambda functions triggered from the API Gateway

A Lambda function integration must be defined for the API Gateway so it can publish events to a Lambda function when it receives HTTP requests. The following steps must be performed to configure a HTTP endpoint on API Gateway:

1. Create a new API.
2. Create the web resource for the endpoint with its name and path. For example /myStore.
3. Create HTTP methods for the resource, such as GET, POST, PUT, DELETE or PATCH.
4. For each method set the Integration Type to Lambda function, select the region and the name of the Lambda function.

When an API Gateway receives HTTP requests it will send events to Amazon Lambda to invoke Lambda functions.

The API Gateway endpoint may be defined using a Swagger definition file.

8.7.1 Swagger Definition File

Swagger (OpenAPI) is a widely used specification for REST APIs. AWS API Gateway supports Swagger. Swagger definition files can be imported into API Gateway to define and configure REST API names, resources and methods. Swagger definition files specify the REST API details in YAML or JSON format. The full OpenAPI specification can be found at:

http://swagger.io/specification/

The Swagger Editor provides a way to edit and evaluate Swagger definitions. A sample Swagger YAML definition file is shown below.

```
swagger: '2.0'
info:
  version: '1.0.0'
  title: Swagger Petstore (Simple)
  description: A simple petstore API.
basePath: /
schemes:
  - http
consumes:
  - application/json
produces:
  - application/json
paths:
  /pets:
    get:
      description: Returns all pets
      operationId: getPets
      produces:
        - application/json
      responses:
        '200':
          description: pet response
          schema:
            type: array
            items:
              $ref: '#/definitions/pet'
        default:
          description: unexpected error
          schema:
            $ref: '#/definitions/errorModel'
  /pets/{id}:
    get:
      description: Get a pet.
      operationId: getPetById
      produces:
        - application/json
      parameters:
        - name: id
          in: path
          description: Pet ID
```

```
          required: true
          type: integer
          format: int64
    responses:
      '200':
        description: pet response
        schema:
          $ref: '#/definitions/pet'
      default:
        description: unexpected error
        schema:
          $ref: '#/definitions/errorModel'
definitions:
  pet:
    type: object
    required:
      - id
      - name
    properties:
      id:
        type: integer
        format: int64
      name:
        type: string
      tag:
        type: string
  newPet:
    type: object
    required:
      - name
    properties:
      id:
        type: integer
        format: int64
      name:
        type: string
      tag:
        type: string
  errorModel:
    type: object
    required:
      - code
      - message
    properties:
      code:
        type: integer
        format: int32
      message:
        type: string
```

API Gateway has extended the Swagger definitions to integrate with a Lambda function by adding `x-amazon-apigateway-integration` as shown in this Swagger YAML snippet.

```
paths:
  /user:
    get:
      responses:
      x-amazon-apigateway-integration:
        type: aws
        uri: arn:aws:apigateway:region:lambda:path/
              2015-03-31/functions/function-name/invocations
        responses:
          default:
            statusCode: 200
```

8.7.2 Integration Configuration

When you create a new API from the AWS Console you can import a Swagger definition file as shown below.

The API Gateway can also be integrated with a Lambda function using the `put-rest-api` CLI command that references a Swagger definition file containing the `x-amazon-apigateway-integration` extension.

```
aws apigateway put-rest-api
            --rest-api-id 1234123412
            --mode overwrite
            --body 'file:///path/to/swagger-definition.json'
            --region region
```

This can be tested using the `test-invoke-method` CLI command:

```
aws apigateway test-invoke-method
            --rest-api-id 1234123412
            --resource-id abc123
            --http-method POST
            --path-with-query-string ""
            --body "{"id": "1", "item-name": "item1"}"
```

8.7.3 API Gateway Blueprints

The 'microservice-http-endpoint' blueprint describes the integration of API Gateway with Lambda functions:

8.8 API Gateway Custom Authorizer

The API Gateway can also use a Lambda function as a custom authorizer to authenticate and authorize incoming requests.

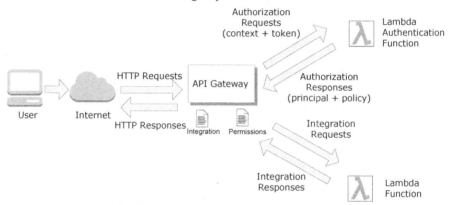

Figure 14: API Gateway Custom Authorization using Lambda Function

The API Gateway is configured with a Lambda function as a custom authorizer. When the API gateway receives a HTTP request it sends a request to the Lambda function with an authorization token extracted from a specified request header. The Lambda function validates the authorization token and produces a policy document. The Lambda function performs the custom authorization by JSON Web Token (JWT) verification, or by calling an OAuth provider.

The AWS Lambda Console includes blueprints to create Lambda functions for custom authorization.

A code snippet for a Python Lambda function that performs authorization is shown below.

```
def lambda_handler(event, context):
    print("Client token: " + event['authorizationToken'])
    print("Method ARN: " + event['methodArn'])

    tmp = event['methodArn'].split(':')
    apiGatewayArnTmp = tmp[5].split('/')
    awsAccountId = tmp[4]

    policy = AuthPolicy(principalId, awsAccountId)
```

```
policy.restApiId = apiGatewayArnTmp[0]
policy.region = tmp[3]
policy.stage = apiGatewayArnTmp[1]
policy.denyAllMethods()

# Build the policy
authResponse = policy.build()

return authResponse
```

8.8.1 Request Data Format

The API Gateway sends an authorization request with an `authorizationToken` parameter containing the token from the HTTP request header. The `type` field must be set to TOKEN.

```
{
    "type":"TOKEN",
    "authorizationToken": caller-supplied-token,
    "methodArn":"arn:aws:executeapi:region:account:<apiId>/stage/
                 method/resource-path"
}
```

8.8.2 Response Data Format

The Lambda function sends an authorization response to the API gateway with a principal identifier `principalId` and a policy document `policyDocument` containing a list of policy statements.

The authorization response is a JSON message shown below. The policy statement contains permissions for a principal (who) to perform an action (what) on a specific resource (which).

```
{
    "principalId": principal-id,
    "policyDocument": {
        "Version": "2012-10-17",
        "Statement": [
            {
                "Action": "execute-api:Invoke",
                "Effect": "Allow|Deny",
                "Resource":
                    arn:aws:execute-api:region:account:api-id/stage-name/
                        http-verb/resourcepath-specifier
            }
        ]
    },
}
```

If the token is valid, a policy is generated to allow or deny access to the client. If access is denied, the client will receive a 403 Access Denied response. If access is allowed, API Gateway will proceed with the backend integration configured on the method that was called.

8.8.3 Custom Authorizer Configuration

The custom authorizer for an API Gateway can be configured from the API Gateway Console. Select Authorizers in the left hand pane.

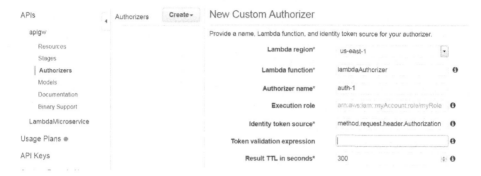

The custom authorizer for an API Gateway can also be configured using the CLI command create-authorizer.

```
aws apigateway create-authorizer
        --rest-api-id 1234123412
        --name authorizer-name
        --type TOKEN
        --authorizer-uri 'arn:aws:apigateway:region:lambda:
            path/2015-03-31/functions/arn:aws:lambda:
            region:account:function:custom-auth-
function/invocations'
        --identity-source 'method.request.header.Authorization'
        --region region
```

8.8.4 API Gateway Authorizer Blueprints

These blueprints describe the integration of API Gateway with a Lambda function custom authorizer:
- api-gateway-authorizer-nodejs. Custom authorizer implemented in Node.js.
- api-gateway-authorizer-python. Custom authorizer implemented in Python.

8.9 Lambda@Edge and CloudFront

CloudFront is a service that delivers static and dynamic content for Web pages through a number of data centers located at the edge of the network. Rather than retrieving content data from the origin servers it is instead cached at the edge data centers and is managed by CloudFront. This provides the lowest latency for delivery of content to the viewer.

Lambda@Edge allows CloudFront to invoke Lambda functions that can customize the content as it is exchanged between the viewer and the content origin server. CloudFront can be configured to invoke Lambda functions when four different HTTP requests are processed:

- When viewer requests are received from a viewer.
- Before responses are sent to the viewer.
- Before requests are sent to the Origin server
- When origin responses are received from the Origin server.

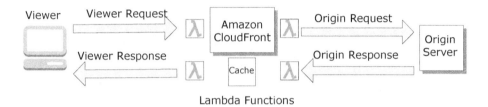

Lambda Functions

Figure 15: Lambda functions triggered from CloudFront

The Lambda function runtime must be set to Edge-Node.js 4.3. Examples of the Node.js requests and responses are shown below.

```
exports.viewer_request_handler = (event, context, callback) => {
  var headers = event.Records[0].cf.request.headers;
  for (var header in headers) {
    /* Custom logic */
  }
  callback(null, event.Records[0].cf_request);
}

exports.viewer_response_handler = (event, context, callback) => {
  var headers = event.Records[0].cf.response.headers;
  for (var header in headers) {
    /* Custom logic */
  }
  callback(null, event.Records[0].cf.response);
}

exports.origin_request_handler = (event, context, callback) => {
  var headers = event.Records[0].cf.request.headers;
  for (var header in headers) {
    /* Custom logic */
  }
  callback(null, event.Records[0].cf_request);
}
```

```
exports.origin_response_handler = (event, context, callback) => {
  var headers = event.Records[0].cf.response.headers;
  for (var header in headers) {
    /* Custom logic */
  }
  callback(null, event.Records[0].cf.response);
}
```

For cross-account access, an IAM Execution Role is required as well as permisson for Lambda@Edge to invoke the Lambda function.

When using the AWS CLI, add the permission shown below. This is done automatically when using the AWS Console.

```
aws lambda add-permission
              --function-name function-arn
              --statement-id statement-id
              --action lambda:GetFunction
              --principal edgelambda.amazonaws.com
```

8.9.1 Input Data Format

An example of the request that CloudFront sends to a Lambda function is shown below:

```
{"Records":[
  {
    "cf": {
      "configuration": {
        "distributionId": "EXAMPLE"
      },
      "request": {
        "uri": "/me.pic",
        "method": "GET",
        "httpVersion": "2.0",
        "clientIp": "2001:cdba::3257:9652",
        "headers": {
          "User-Agent": ["Test Agent"],
          "Host": ["d2fadu0nynjpfn.cloudfront.net"]
        }
      }
    }
  }
]}
```

An example of the response that CloudFront sends to a Lambda function is shown below:

```
{"Records":[
  {
    "cf": {
```

```
    "configuration": {
      "distributionId": "EXAMPLE "
    },
    "response": {
      "status": "200",
      "statusDescription": "HTTP OK",
      "httpVersion": "2.0",
      "headers": {
        "User-agent": ["mozilla", "safari"],
        "Vary": ["*"]
      }
    }
  }
]}
```

8.9.2 Trigger Configuration

To create Lambda@Edge functions that will be triggered from CloudFront use the AWS Management Console. Use the following steps:

1. Choose Create a Lambda function.
2. In Select blueprint, choose a CloudFront blueprint such as cloudfront-modify-response-header.

This blueprint will automatically select a CloudFront trigger for the Lambda function.

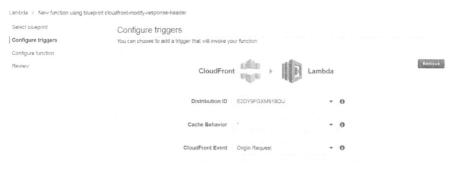

3. Next, configure the Lambda function. Enter its name, and description. The runtime must be Edge Node.js 4.3. Modify the code in the code panel as desired.

Lambda > New function using blueprint cloudfront-modify-response-header

Select blueprint

Configure triggers

Configure function

Review

Configure function

A Lambda function consists of the custom code you want to execute. Learn more about Lambda functions.

Name*   cfRequest

Description   Blueprint for modifying CloudFront response

Runtime*   Edge Node.js 4.3

Lambda function code

4. Enter the Lambda function handler execution role. Start by using an existing role: `lambda_basic_execution`.

5. Next review the Lambda function configuration before clicking on the Create Function button. The main Lambda function management window is now displayed. This window has a number of panes: Code, Configuration, Triggers and Monitoring.

8.9.3 CloudFront Blueprints

There are several blueprints for the integration of CloudFront with Lambda functions:

- cloudfront-modify-response-header. Modifies a response header, implemented in Node.js.
- cloudfront-ab-test. CloudFront ab testing, implemented in Node.js.
- cloudfront-http-redirect. Returns an HTTP redirect, implemented in Node.js.
- cloudfront-response-generation. Generates a response from viewer-request trigger, implemented in Node.js.

8.10 CloudWatch Scheduled Events

AWS CloudWatch may be used to send regular scheduled events to Lambda functions. A CloudWatch rule can be created to specify the schedule expression and the ARN of the Lambda function.

Other CloudWatch events can be triggered for other services, such as Auto-scaling life-cycle events which are triggered on the launch or termination of an EC2 instance.

For cross-account access, an IAM Execution Role is required as well as permisson for CloudWatch to invoke the Lambda function.

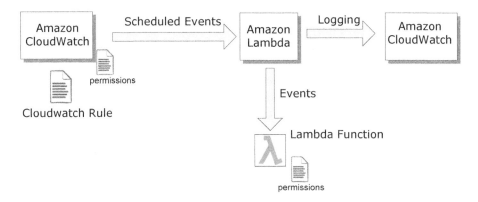

Figure 16: Lambda functions scheduled from CloudWatch

8.10.1 Input Data Format

CloudWatch sends scheduled events to a Lambda function with a JSON message structure shown below:

```
{
  "account": account,
  "region": region,
  "detail": {},
  "detail-type": "Scheduled Event",
  "source": "aws.events",
  "time": "1970-01-01T00:00:00Z",
  "id": "EVENT-ID",
  "resources": [
    "arn:aws:events:region:account:rule/schedule-rule"
  ]
}
```

8.10.2 Trigger Configuration

A CloudWatch rule to schedule a Lambda function is configured using the AWS Management Console or by using CloudWatch CLI commands. The scheduling can be done using `rate` or `cron` expressions.

The rate expression has the form: `rate(value unit)`

- `value` must be a positive integer, and `unit` must be either minute(s), hour(s), or day(s).
- The minimum rate duration is 1 minute.

- A singular value must have the singular tense of the unit and, likewise, plural values must have the plural tense of the unit.

For example, `rate(1 hour)` triggers a Lambda function every 1 hour, and `rate(5 minutes)` triggers the function every 5 minutes.

The cron expression has the form:
`cron(minutes hours day-of-month month day-of-week year)`

- All time is referenced against UTC.
- All fields are required.
- One of the day-of-month or day-of-week values must be a question mark (?)

For example, `cron(0/15 * * * ? *)` triggers a Lambda function at 0, 15, 30, and 45 minutes past the hour, every hour of every day.

Click on CloudWatch in the AWS Management Console and select Events and Rules. Next, set the Event Source to Schedule and choose either a fixed duration or a Cron expression. Finally, select the Lambda function as an event target.

Use the CloudWatch CLI command `put-rule` to configure a scheduled event.

```
aws events put-rule --name rule-name
                    --schedule-expression 'rate(X minutes)'
```

Use the CloudWatch CLI command `put-targets` to add the Lambda function to this rule:

```
aws events put-targets --rule rule-name
                       --targets file://targets.json
```

The JSON file `targets.json` specifies a Lambda function as the target.

```
[{
  "Id": "1",
  "Arn": "arn:aws:lambda:region:account:
```

```
                       function:scheduled-function"
}]
```

8.11 CloudFormation

AWS CloudFormation is used to create and configure AWS resources such as Amazon EC2 instances or Amazon S3 instances. A collection of resources is called a stack. CloudFormation stacks are specified using CloudFormation Templates (CFT) which represent the resources that make up a CloudFormation stack in JSON or YAML format. The AWS CloudFormer tool can be used to create a CloudFormation stack from existing resources in your account.

A Lambda function can be invoked on the creation, update, or deletion of CloudFormation stacks.

For cross-account access, an IAM Execution Role is required as well as permisson for CloudWatch to invoke the Lambda function.

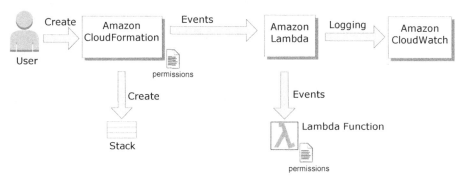

Figure 17: Lambda functions triggered from CloudFormation

8.11.1 Input Data Format

CloudFormation sends events to a Lambda function with a JSON message structure shown below:

```
{
  "StackId": stack-id-arn,
  "ResourceProperties": {
    "ServiceToken":
      "arn:aws:lambda:region:account:function:lambda-function",
    "StackName": "TestStack",
    "Region": region
  },
  "RequestType": "Create",
  "ResourceType": "Custom::TestResourceType",
  "RequestId": unique-id,
  "LogicalResourceId": "TestResource"
```

```
}
```

8.11.2 Trigger Configuration

A CloudFormation resource can be configured to trigger a Lambda function. A custom resource is created with Type starting with the word `Custom::` followed by a user-defined suffix, such as `Custom::TestResourceType`. The resource must have a `ServiceToken` property with its value being the ARN of the Lambda function. Other properties of the resource are passed to the Lambda function in the triggering event data.

```
"Resources": {
  "TestResource": {
    "Type": "Custom::TestResourceType",
    "Properties": {
      "ServiceToken":
        "arn:aws:lambda:region:account:function:lambda-function",
      "StackName": "TestStack",
      "Region": {"Ref:" "AWS::Region"}
    }
  }
}
```

8.12 AWS Config

The AWS Config service provides an inventory of all AWS resources associated with an AWS account. It also journals all resource configuration changes and makes this information available through an API. AWS Config manages configuration items for AWS resources.

AWS Config provides a Config Rules capability where rules can be written to validate a configuration item for an AWS resource. These may be predefined rules provided by AWS, or they may be custom rules provided by Lambda functions.

The Lambda function uses the AWS Config `putEvaluations` SDK call to return the result of the configuration to AWS Config as shown below.

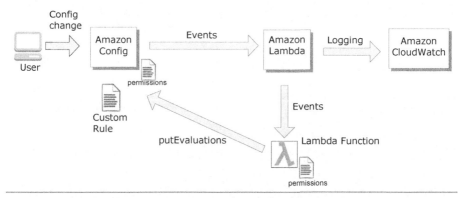

Figure 18: Lambda functions triggered from AWS Config Custom Rule

8.12.1 Trigger Configuration

Custom rules for AWS Config are evaluated using associated Lambda functions. The association may be done using the AWS Management Console or by using a AWS Config service CLI command.

The AWS Config CLI command `put-config-rule` may be used to configure a trigger to invoke a Lambda function.

```
aws configservice put-config-rule
                  --config-rule file:config-rule.json
```

The JSON formatted rule configuration file is shown below.

```
{
  "ConfigRuleName": "CustomLambdaRule",
  "Description": "Custom evaluation rule.",
  "Scope": {
    "ComplianceResourceTypes": [
      "AWS::EC2::Instance"
    ]
  },
  "Source": {
    "Owner": "CUSTOM_LAMBDA",
    "SourceIdentifier":
      "arn:aws:lambda:region:account:function:LambdaEvaluation",
    "SourceDetails": [
      {
        "EventSource": "aws.config",
        "MessageType": "ConfigurationItemChangeNotification"
      }
    ]
  },
  "InputParameters": ""
}
```

8.13 CodeCommit

AWS CodeCommit is a source code control service that is used to host secure, private Git repositories. Triggers can be added to a CodeCommit repository so that when it is updated by a code commit, an event is sent to a Lambda function. The creation or deletion of branches or tags in the repository can also trigger events to a Lambda function.

Cross-account access from CodeCommit to Lambda functions requires two sets of permissions:

1. IAM Execution Role for the Lambda function itself.

2. CodeCommit permission to invoke the Lambda function.

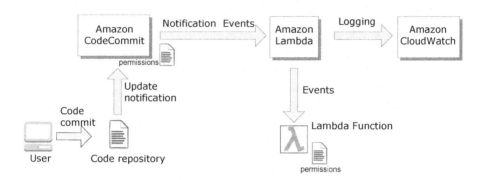

Figure 19: Lambda functions triggered from CodeCommit

8.13.1 Trigger Configuration

CodeCommit triggers for Lambda functions may be configured using the AWS Management Console or by using a CodeCommit CLI command.

The CodeCommit CLI command `put-repository-triggers` may be used to configure a trigger on a repository to invoke a Lambda function.

```
aws codecommit put-repository-triggers -
               -cli-input-json file:trigger.json
```

This command uses a JSON file to specify the trigger. This file includes the following:

- The repository and branches that will initiate the trigger.
- The ARN of the target Lambda function.
- The CodeCommit events that will initiate this trigger. These include:
  - Commits updated to the repository.
  - A new branch or tag created in the repository.
  - A branch or tag deleted in the repository.

An example of the JSON file is shown below.

```
{
  "repositoryName": repository-name,
  "triggers": [
    {
      "name": trigger-name,
      "destinationArn":
        "arn:aws:lambda:region:account:function:function-name",
      "customData": "",
      "branches": [
        "branch1", "branch2"
```

```
      ],
      "events": [
        "updateReference"
      ]
    }
  ]
}
```

8.14 Alexa Cloud Service

The Alexa Cloud Service receives audio streams from devices such as the Alexa Echo or the Alexa Dot and transforms them into commands. The Alexa Cloud Service uses the Alexa Skills Kit (ASK) to send the transformed audio data, as Intent Schema requests, to a Lambda function.

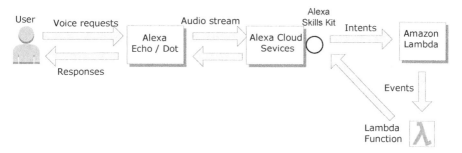

Figure 20: Lambda functions triggered from Alexa Cloud Services

8.14.1 Input Data Format

The Alexa Intent events have a JSON message structure. A customized Intent structure is used to send the transformed audio data to the Lambda function. Alexa sends a number of standard intents to the Lambda function in addition to customized intents:

- AMAZON.HelpIntent: to provide the user with help text
- AMAZON.StopIntent: to let the user stop an operation
- AMAZON.CancelIntent: to let the user cancel an operation

The Lambda function must accept and respond to three different types of requests:

- LaunchRequest
- IntentRequest
- SessionEndedRequest

An example of an `IntentRequest` sent to the Lambda function is shown below. Each `intent` structure has a `slots` parameter which contains utterance information.

```
{
  "session": {
    "sessionId": session-id,
    "application": {
      "applicationId": app-id
    },
    "attributes": {},
    "user": {
      "userId": user-id
    },
    "new": true
  },
  "request": {
    "type": "IntentRequest",
    "requestId": request-id,
    "locale": "en-US",
    "timestamp": "2017-01-23T21:02:05Z",
    "intent": {
      "name": "GetSundown",
      "slots": {
        "Weekday": {
          "name": "Weekday",
          "value": "Monday"
        }
      }
    }
  },
  "version": "1.0"
}
```

8.14.2 Trigger Configuration

Alexa Skills Kit trigger configuration for Lambda functions may be done using the AWS Developer Console. Follow these steps to setup the Alexa to Lambda function integration:

1. Log in to your account and select Getting Started with the Alexa Skills Kit.

Get started with Alexa

Add new voice-enabled capabilities using the Alexa Skills Kit, or add voice-powered experiences to your connected devices with the Alexa Voice Service.

Alexa Skills Kit
Easily add new skills to Alexa
Get Started >

Alexa Voice Service
Bring voice capabilities to your connected device
Get Started >

2. Click on Create New Skill and enter the skill information including its type, name and invocation name. Then click on the Next button.

3. Enter the interaction model information including the Intent schema, any custom slot types and some sample utterances.

4. Associate the Alexa skill with the ARN of the Lambda function.

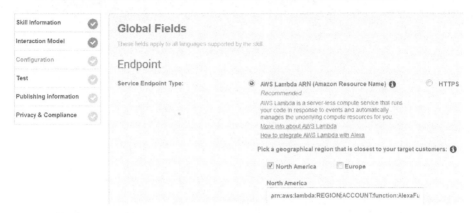

5. Test the interaction between the Alexa skill and the Lambda function using the Alexa Service simulator.

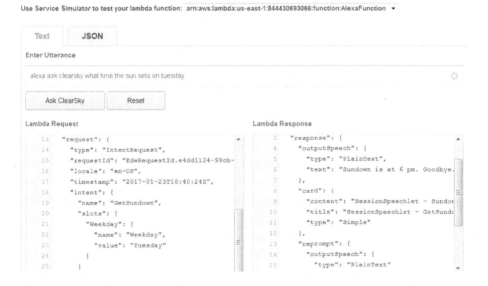

6. Once the testing is complete and you are satisfied with the Alexa skill, it must be submitted for certification so it can be published and be available to users. The skill must be compliant with Alexa policy and security guidelines.

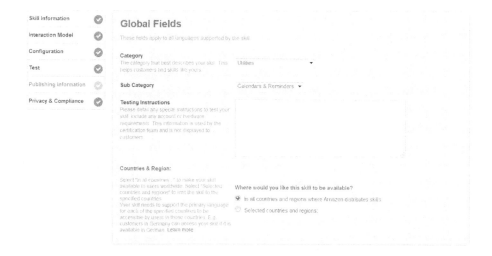

8.15 AWS Lex

AWS Lex is a speech recognition and natural language understanding service that can be used to build conversational interfaces for applications. Lambda functions can be triggered from AWS Lex.

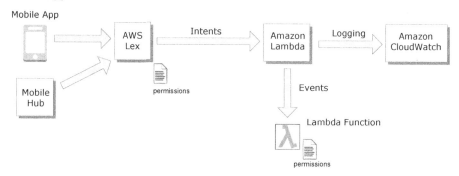

Figure 21: Lambda functions triggered from AWS Lex

8.15.1 Input Data Format

AWS Lex sends events to a Lambda function with a JSON message structure shown below:

```
{
   "messageVersion": "1.0",
   "invocationSource": fulfillment-code-hook or dialog-code-hook,
   "userId": "user-id specified in the POST request to Amazon
Lex.",
   "sessionAttributes": {
```

```
      "key1":  "value1",
      "key2":  "value2",
    },
    "bot": {
      "name": bot-name,
      "alias": bot-alias,
      "version": bot-version
    },
    "outputDialogMode":  "Text or Voice",
    "currentIntent": {
      "name": intent-name,
      "slots": {
        "slot-name": slot-name,
      },
      "confirmationStatus":  "None, Confirmed, or Denied"
  }
```

8.16 AWS IoT

AWS Internet of Things (IoT) is a service that provides secure, reliable communication between Internet connected devices and services in the AWS cloud.

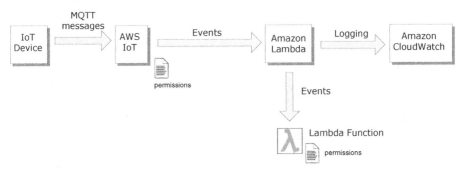

Figure 22: Lambda functions triggered from IoT

The AWS IoT Message Broker receives messages from IoT devices that have been published in JSON format to MQTT topics. These messages are used to update an IoT Device Shadow which maintains the current state of the IoT devices.

The IoT Rules Engine includes rules that can be used to filter the messages and actions to deliver notification events to AWS services such as Lambda functions. The AWS IoT Rules Engine matches incoming MQTT messages against the filter conditions of a rule. When a matching message is received, the rule action invokes a Lambda function with the data in the MQTT message from the IoT device.

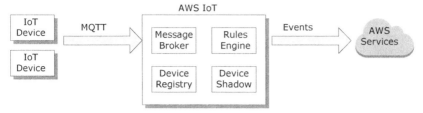

Figure 23: AWS IoT Service

8.16.1 Trigger Configuration

An AWS IoT rule consists of a SQL SELECT statement, a topic filter, and a rule action.. The SQL SELECT statement specifies the incoming MQTT message. The topic filter of an AWS IoT rule specifies one or more MQTT topics. The rule is triggered when an MQTT message is received on a topic that matches the topic filter. Rule actions allow you to take the information extracted from an MQTT message and send it to another AWS service.

A rule may be created using the IoT CLI `create-topic-rule` command:

```
aws iot create-topic-rule --rule-name rule-name
                          --topic-rule-payload file://rule.json
```

The contents of the JSON rule file are shown in the example below. The Lambda action of the rule references the ARN of a Lambda function.

```
{
    "sql": "SELECT * FROM 'building1/fan/'",
    "ruleDisabled": false,
    "actions": [{
        "lambda": {
            "functionArn":
                "arn:aws:lambda:region:account:function:lambda-function"
        }
    }]
}
```

8.17 AWS Mobile SDK

AWS Lambda functions can be called directly from mobile applications using the Mobile SDK.

For the Mobile SDK to invoke a Lambda function requires two sets of permissions:

1. IAM Execution Role for the Lambda function itself

2. Mobile SDK permission to invoke the Lambda function. The Amazon Cognito service can be used to manage user identities, authentication, and permissions.

An Android mobile application can call Lambda functions using the Mobile SDK for Android with the `aws-android-sdk-lambda` library. The SDK first sends a request to AWS Cognito with its identity, and then Cognito generates the credentials and returns them to the SDK. Next the SDK invokes the Lambda function. On invocation, the context object includes data about the device, application and the end user identity.

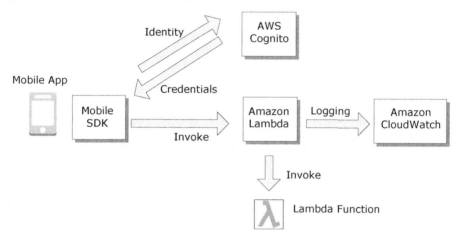

Figure 24: Lambda Function triggered from Android Mobile SDK

8.17.1 Trigger Configuration

Client methods in an Android Java application can be mapped to Lambda function invocations, using the `@LambdaFunction` annotation. For example, the code below will result in the `LambdaBackendFunction` Lambda function being executed every time the `LambdaBackendFunction` method is called inside the application code.

```
@LambdaFunction
ResponseClass LambdaBackendFunction(RequestClass request);
```

The `@LambdaFunction` annotation has optional parameters: `functionName`, `invocationType` and `LogType`.

Use the `functionName` parameter to specify the name of the Lambda function to call when the method is executed. Use `invocationType` to specify how the Lambda function will be invoked: `Event`, `RequestResponse` and `DryRun`. If the `LogType` parameter is set to `Tail`, AWS Lambda will return the last 4KB of log data from the Lambda Function in the `x-amz-log-results` header, which is base64-encoded. This parameter is valid only when invocationType is set to `RequestResponse`.

```
@LambdaFunction(functionName = "functionA",
```

```
                invocationType = "Event",
                logType = "Tail")
RequestClass FunctionB(RequestClass request);
```

The class containing methods with the @LambdaFunction annotation must be instantiated using the lambdainvoker.LambdaInvokerFactory.Build() method.

8.17.2 Lambda Function Example

Lambda functions can access data about the device and the mobile application using the context object passed to the handler using context.clientContext and context.identity as shown in the Node.js example below.

```
exports.handler = function(event, context) {
  console.log("installation_id = " +
              context.clientContext.client.installation_id);
  console.log("app_version_code = " +
              context.clientContext.client.app_version_code);
  console.log("app_version_name = " +
              context.clientContext.client.app_version_name);
  console.log("app_package_name = " +
              context.clientContext.client.app_package_name);
  console.log("app_title = " +
              context.clientContext.client.app_title);
  console.log("platform_version = " +
              context.clientContext.env.platform_versioin);
  console.log("platform = " +
context.clientContext.env.platform);
  console.log("make = " + context.clientContext.env.make);
  console.log("model = " + context.clientContext.env.model);
  console.log("locale = " + context.clientContext.env.locale);
}
```

8.18 AWS Cognito

AWS Cognito Sync provides the ability to sync user data between different devices such as mobile phones or tablets. Cognito stores user data in datasets as key-value pairs. The user data is associated with an Amazon Cognito identity.

Amazon Cognito Events will send a Sync Trigger event to a Lambda function when a user updates their data. The Sync trigger event contains all the records from the updated dataset.

The Lambda function can then evaluate and optionally manipulate the data before it is stored in the cloud and synchronized to the user's other devices. Cognito expects that the return value of the Lambda function is in the same JSON format as the input.

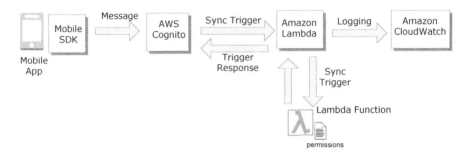

Figure 25: Cognito Sync Trigger Events

8.18.1 Trigger Configuration

Cognito Event Sync triggers for Lambda functions may be configured using the AWS Cognito console. Select 'Edit identity pool' in the Federated Identity screen and then in the Cognito Events section, select the Lambda function to be invoked for the Sync Trigger

▾ Cognito Events

Cognito Events allow developers to run an AWS Lambda function in response to important events in Cognito. Learn more about Cognito Events.

Sync Trigger ❶   LambdaFoo ▾

The Cognito Identity CLI command `list-identity-pools` may also be used to list the pools.

```
aws cognito-identity list-identity-pools --max-results 10
{
  "IdentityPools": [
    {
    "IdentityPoolId": identity-pool-id,
    "IdentityPoolName": "myApp"
    }
  ]
}
```

The Cognito Sync CLI command `set-cognito-events` may also be used to configure a Sync trigger on a specific Cognito Identity pool.

```
aws cognito-sync set-cognito-events
              --identity-pool-id pool-id
              --events event-map
```

8.18.2 Input Data Format

AWS Cognito sends Sync Trigger events to a Lambda function with a JSON message structure shown below.

```
{
  "version": 2,
  "eventType": "SyncTrigger",
  "region": "us-east-1",
  "identityPoolId": "identityPoolId",
  "identityId": "identityId",
  "datasetName": "datasetName",
  "datasetRecords": {
    "SampleKey1": {
      "oldValue": "oldValue1",
      "newValue": "newValue1",
      "op": "replace"
    },
    "SampleKey2": {
      "oldValue": "oldValue2",
      "newValue": "newValue2",
      "op": "replace"
    }
  }
}
```

Records updated by the user will have the `op` field set as `replace` and the records deleted will have `op` field as `remove`. The Lambda function can modify any record as follows:

- To modify the value of a record, update the value and set the `op` to `replace`.
- To remove a record, either set the `op` to `remove`, or set the value to null.
- To add a record, simply add a new record to the `datasetRecords` array.

8.18.3 Lambda Function Example

An example of a Node.js Lambda function that processes a Sync trigger event is shown below.

```
exports.handler = function(event, context) {
  console.log(JSON.stringify(event, null, 2));
  //Check for the event type
  if (event.eventType === 'SyncTrigger') {
    //Modify value for a key
    if('SampleKey1' in event.datasetRecords){
      event.datasetRecords.SampleKey1.newValue = 'ModifyValue1';
      event.datasetRecords.SampleKey1.op = 'replace';
    }
    //Remove a key
    if('SampleKey2' in event.datasetRecords){
```

```
      event.datasetRecords.SampleKey2.op = 'remove';
    }
    //Add a key
    if(!('SampleKey3' in event.datasetRecords)){
      event.datasetRecords.SampleKey3={'newValue':'ModifyValue3',
                                        'op' : 'replace'};
    }
  }
  context.done(null, event);
};
```

8.18.4 Cognito Blueprints

The 'cognito-sync-trigger' blueprint describes the integration of Cognito with
Lambda functions.

8.19 Multiple Event Sources

A Lambda function can process events from more the one source. The JSON
message structure is used to discriminate between different event sources as shown
in this Node.js snippet which handles events from Kinesis and S3 event sources:

```
exports.handler = function(event, context) {
  var record = event.Records[0];
  if (record.kinesis) {
    exports.kinesisHandler(event.Records, context);
  } else if (record.s3) {
    exports.s3Handler(record, context);
  }
};
```

9 Invoking Services from Lambda

Lambda functions can invoke other AWS services or external non-AWS services.

9.1 AWS Services

Lambda functions can invoke other AWS services by using the APIs provides by those other AWS services. Here are some examples of how this is done.

9.1.1 Invoking another Lambda Function

In this example a Python Lambda function invokes another Lambda function that uses the boto3 Lambda client library. The on-demand asynchronous invocation of the other Lambda function is specified using the `Event InvocationType`, so that the invoking Lambda function does not accrue billing charges waiting for the invoked Lambda function to finish executing.

```
from boto3 import client as boto3_client
from datetime import datetime
import json

lambda_client = boto3_client('lambda')

def lambda_handler(event, context):
    msg = {"key":"invocation", "at": datetime.now()}
    invoke_response =
        lambda_client.invoke(FunctionName=lambda-function-name,
                             InvocationType='Event',
                             Payload=json.dumps(msg))
    print(invoke_response)
```

It is also possible to chain Lambda functions via SNS. One Lambda function publishes messages to an SNS topic and a second Lambda function is subscribed to this topic. When a message arrives at the SNS topic, the second Lambda function is triggered with the message as its input event.

9.1.2 Invoking Time Service

This is an example of a Node.js Lambda function requesting time.

```
var time = require('time');
exports.handler = (event, context, callback) => {
  var currentTime = new time.Date();
  currentTime.setTimezone("America/Los_Angeles");
  callback(null, {
    statusCode: '200', body: 'The time is: ' +
                            currentTime.toString(),
  });
```

```
};
```

9.1.3 Invoking SNS Service

A Lambda function can also be written to publish to a SNS topic by referencing the ARN of the SNS topic as shown below.

```
var AWS = require('aws-sdk');

var message = {};
var sns = new AWS.SNS();
sns.publish({
  TopicArn: sns-topic-arn,
  Message: JSON.stringify(message)
},)
```

9.1.4 Invoking S3 Service

This is an example of a Java Lambda function writing to an S3 object.

```
public Response handleRequest(Request request, Context context) {
  AmazonS3Client s3Client = new AmazonS3Client();
  S3Object = s3Client.getObject("object", request.getFilename());
  ....
  return new Response(result);
}
```

This is an example of a Node.js Lambda function writing to an S3 object.

```
var AWS = require('aws-sdk');
var s3 = new AWS.S3();
exports.handler = function(event, context) {
  //console.log(JSON.stringify(event, null, 2));
  var s3 = new AWS.S3();
  console.log("s3");
  s3.upload(param, function(err, data) {
      if (err) console.log(err, err.stack); // an error occurred
      else console.log(data);              // successful response

      console.log('actually done!');
      context.done();
  });

  console.log('done?');
  //context.done();
};
```

9.1.5 Invoking DynamoDB Service

This is an example of a Node.js Lambda function writing to a DynamoDB table.

```
var aws = require('aws-sdk');
var dynamo = new AWS.DynamoDB.DocumentClient({region: 'us-west-
2'});

exports.handler = function(event, context) {
    var file_path = ...
    var gallery = ...

    var params = {
        TableName: 'ddb-name',
        Item: {
            gallery: gallery,
            file_path: file_path
        }
    };
    dynamo.put(params, context.done);
};
```

9.2 External Services

9.2.1 Invoking IFFFT Maker

Lambda functions can also invoke external service such as an IFFFT Maker channel. IFTTT (If This Then That) is a free Internet-based service that lets you create chains of simple conditional statements called applets.

This snippet of code shows a Node.js Lambda function sending an HTTP request to an IFTTT Maker channel.

```
AWS.config.update({region: region});
var IFTTTkey = key;
var request = require('request');

exports.handler = function(event, context) {
  request('https://maker.ifttt.com/trigger/' +
          'AWS-'+ buttonState + '/with/key/' + IFTTTkey,
          function (error, response, body) {
              console.log("Response: ", response.statusCode);
          }
)};
```

10 Lambda Functions and VPC

10.1 VPC Introduction

AWS networks typically use the Virtual Private Cloud (VPC) service to control access to services within the cloud. The VPC service provides customers the ability to provision separate, private virtual networks in the AWS cloud to launch resources such as EC2 instances or the RDS database instances. Each VPC is completely isolated from other VPCs in the AWS cloud.

The IP address range of each VPC network may be configured and a VPC network may be partitioned into subnets. EC2 instances and other AWS services can be launched on the subnets of the VPC. For example, a VPC may be created with a public subnet with web server EC2 instances that is accessible from the Internet, and private subnets with RDS DB instances, that is isolated from the Internet.

A public subnet requires an Internet Gateway that allows it to route traffic to the Internet. A private subnet cannot route directly to the Internet, instead it has routes to a NAT Gateway in the public subnet.

Route tables, network gateways, security groups and ACLs may also be configured in VPC. Refer to AWS documentation on a complete description of the AWS VPC service.

10.2 Access to AWS Resources in a VPC

By default, Lambda functions are executed within a VPC managed by the Lambda system and these Lambda functions cannot access resources in a private VPC created by a customer. A Lambda function must be configured with a security group and subnets for that customer VPC to allow it to access resources within that VPC. AWS resources in a customer VPC may include as RDS instances, ElastiCache clusters and Redshift data warehouses.

In the example below, the Lambda function must be created with the VpcConfig parameter that includes the subnet IDs and security group Ids to allow access to the EC2 service within Subnet 1.

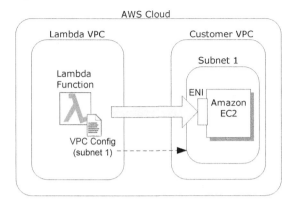

Figure 26: Lambda function access to resources in a Customer VPC

This is used by the Lambda system to set up EC2 Elastic Network Interfaces (ENI) that enables the Lambda function to connect to other resources within a private VPC. An ENI is a virtual network interface attached to EC2 instance in the VPC. ENIs can be created, deleted, as well as attached to and detached from an EC2 instance.

Lambda role must have policy allowing it to create and delete ENIs. AWS provdes a managed policy called `AWSLambdaVPCAccessExecutionRole` to do this.

The VPC configuration for a Lambda function can be specified when it is created or when its configuration is updated. The `create-function` CLI command has the `--vpc-config` parameter to specify the VPC information:

```
aws lambda create-function
  --function-name ExampleFunction
  --runtime python2.7
  --role execution-role-arn
  --zip-file fileb://path/lambda-function.zip
  --handler app.handler
  --vpc-config SubnetIds=vpc-subnet-ids,
            SecurityGroupIds=security-group-ids
  --profile adminuser
```

The `update-function-configuration` CLI command has the `--vpc-config` parameter to add VPC information to an existing Lambda function configuration.

```
aws lambda update-function-configuration
  --function-name function-name
  --vpc-config SubnetIds=vpc-subnet-ids,
            SecurityGroupIds=security-group-ids
```

VPC-related information may be removed from the Lambda function configuration using the `update-function-configuration` CLI command with an empty list of subnet IDs and security group IDs as shown below.

```
aws lambda update-function-configuration
   --function-name function-name
   --vpc-config SubnetIds=[],SecurityGroupIds=[]
```

To allow a Lambda function to access VPC resources, ensure that the VPC has sufficient ENI capacity to support the scaling requirements of the Lambda function. The required ENI capacity is computed as follows:

ENIs used = Concurrent Lambda function executions x
(Lambda function Memory in GB / 1.5GB)

Concurrent Lambda function executions = events/requests per second x
function duration

The VPC subnets should have sufficient available IP addresses to match the number of ENIs to that the scaling of Lambda functions is not limited. The total number of available IP addresses across all subnets must match the number of ENIs.

To allow Lambda functions access to AWS resources in high availability mode, several Availability Zones should be configured with at least one subnet in each AZ so that if one AZ fails the Lambda functions will continue to operate.

10.3 Access to DynamoDB

A DynamoDB resource is not in a VPC and must be treated as a resource in the public Internet. The Lambda function must therefore have access to public Internet. To do so, a NAT gateway and an Internet gateway are needed to provide access to the public Internet. Routes (0.0.0.0/0) must be added to the VPC Route tables to enable traffic from a Lambda function in a private subnet to flow to the NAT Gateway in a public subnet and then to DynamoDB via the Internet Gateway.

For a Lambda function to access the Internet, it must be associated with a private subnet that has Internet access through a VPC NAT gateway configured on a public subnet.

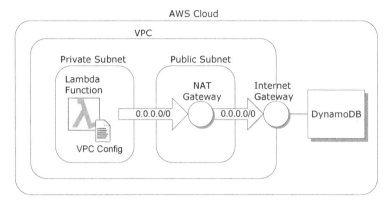

Figure 27: DynamoDB Access from Lambda Functions

10.4 VPC Service Endpoints

The VPC Service Endpoint is a new feature that provides a convenient means of accessing AWS services from VPCs without having to use a NAT gateway as described in the previous section. Lambda functions can use a VPC Service Endpoint to communicate directly with the AWS S3 service.

The Lambda function must be configured with a security group and a subnet of a VPC that has an S3 VPC Service Endpoint.

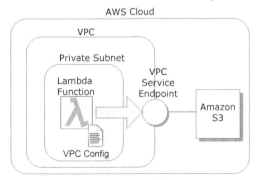

Figure 28: S3 access via VPC Endpoint

A Service Endpoint is created from the VPC dashboard by selecting Endpoints on the left-hand navigation pane.

11 Configuring Lambda Functions

Although Lambda functions can be managed by calls to the Lambda function API, AWS also provides the following set of tools that can be used to configure and manage any AWS service. These tools include:

- AWS Console. This AWS Console lets you manually create and configure Lambda functions using a GUI.

- AWS CLI. This AWS CLI lets you manually create and configure Lambda functions using a CLI command interface.

- AWS SDKs. The SDKs provides a programmatic interface for configuring and managing Lambda functions from applications in a variety of languages.

- AWS Serverless Application Model (SAM) templates. CloudFormation templates provide an easy mechanism for automatically declaring and deploying Lambda Fuunctions and other AWS services in a production environment.

All these tools interact with the AWS services through their APIs as shown in Figure 29.

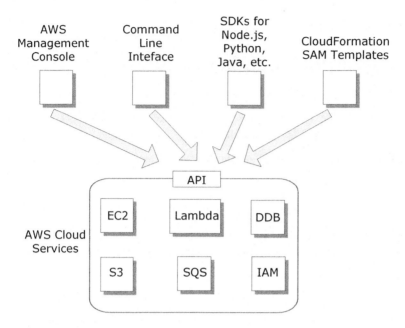

Figure 29: AWS Management Tools

12 AWS Management Console

The AWS Management Console is a web-based GUI that can be accessed using any browser. The AWS Management Console is an easy way to learn about and explore the capabilities of Lambda functions and Step Functions.

Once you have created an AWS account, the AWS Management Console is the dashboard that may be use to manage any AWS service. After logging into the AWS Management Console you are presented with a menu of AWS services as shown below.

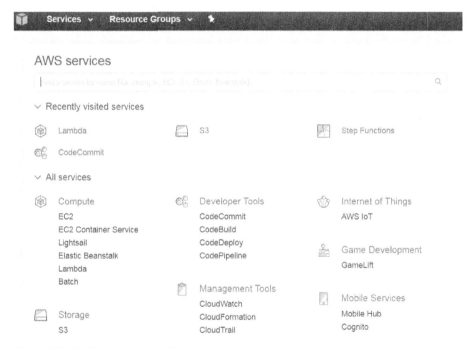

Figure 30: AWS Management Console

A Lambda function may be created using the AWS Management Console. Login to the AWS Management Console and open the AWS Lambda console.

12.1 Creating Lambda Functions

Use the following steps to create a Lambda function:

1. Choose Create a Lambda function.
2. In Select blueprint, choose the Blank Function blueprint.

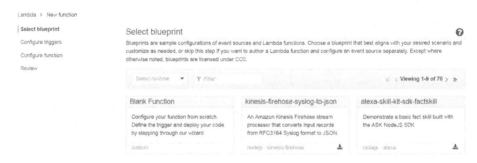

Optionally select the triggers for the Lambda function clicking on the dashed box and choosing a trigger. Some of the triggers include:

- API Gateway
- AWS IoT
- CloudFront
- CloudWatch Scheduled Events
- CloudWatch Logs
- CodeCommit
- Cognito Sync Trigger
- DynamoDB Update
- Kinesis
- S3
- SNS
- Alexa

3. Next, configure the Lambda function. Enter its name, and description. Choose a runtime. Then add code to code template for the blueprint in the code panel.

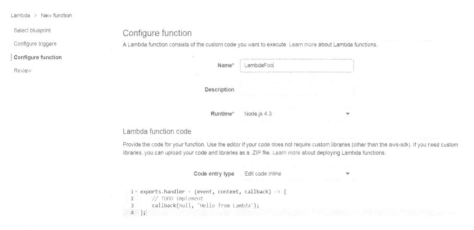

4. Enter the Lambda function handler execution role. Start by using an existing role: `lambda_basic_execution`. Environment variables may also be configured for the Lambda function.

You can define Environment Variables as key-value pairs that are accessible from your function code. These are useful to store configuration settings without the need to change function code. Learn more. For storing sensitive information, we recommend encrypting values using KMS and the console's encryption helpers.

Enable encryption helpers	

Environment variables	Key	Value	✕

Lambda function handler and role

Handler*	index.handler ❶
Role*	Choose an existing role ▾ ❶
Existing role*	lambda_basic_execution ▾ ❶

Advanced settings

These settings allow you to control the code execution performance and costs for your Lambda function. Changing your resource settings (by selecting memory) or changing the timeout may impact your function cost. Learn more about how Lambda pricing works.

Memory (MB)*	128 ▾ ❶

5. Advanced settings such as memory used by the Lambda function, its maximum time duration, dead letter queue, VPC and KMS key may also be configured.

Timeout*	0 ⬍ min 3 ⬍ sec

AWS Lambda will automatically retry failed executions for asynchronous invocations. You can additionally optionally configure Lambda to forward payloads that were not processed to a dead-letter queue (DLQ), such as an SQS queue or an SNS topic. Learn more about Lambda's retry policy and DLQs. **Please ensure your role has appropriate permissions to access the DLQ resource.**

DLQ Resource	Select resource ▾ ❶

All AWS Lambda functions run securely inside a default system-managed VPC. However, you can optionally configure Lambda to access resources, such as databases, within your custom VPC. Learn more about accessing VPCs within Lambda. **Please ensure your role has appropriate permissions to configure VPC.**

VPC	No VPC ▾ ❶

Environment variables are encrypted at rest using a default Lambda service key. You can change the key below to one of your account's keys or paste in a full KMS key ARN.

KMS key	(default) aws/lambda ▾ ❶

* These fields are required.   Cancel   Previous   Next

6. Next review the Lambda function configuration before clicking on the Create Function button. The main Lambda function management window is now displayed. This window has a number of panes: Code, Configuration, Triggers and Monitoring.

7. This window can also be used to test the Lambda function, modify qualifiers, set the test event, publish the Lambda function, create an alias, delete and export the Lambda function.

12.2 Testing Lambda Functions

Use the following steps to test a Lambda function and inspect the results of the invocation:

1. Click on the Test button to run a test. A dialog box is displayed that can be used to configure the test event that is passed as input to the Lambda function. The test event is a set of key-value pairs in JSON format.

2. Click on the Save and Test button to initiate the test. The Summary panel displays the test results including duration, billed duration and resources used. The Log output panel displays the logging output generated by the Lambda function.

12.3 Monitoring Lambda Functions

The Lambda function console provides a summary of its execution metrics, and CloudWatch can be used to view the detailed logs and metrics generated by a Lambda function.

1. Click on the Lambda function Monitoring tab to display a summary of its CloudWatch metrics. Panels showing Invocations, Duration, Errors and Throttles are displayed. The duration shows minimum, maximum, and average time of execution of the Lambda function in milliseconds.

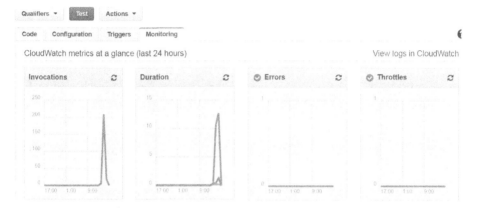

2. Click on View logs in CloudWatch to see the list of CloudWatch log streams for the Lambda function. Note that it may take several seconds before the log streams appear on the CloudWatch console.

3. Click on an individual log to view the logging details.

4. Lambda function metrics can also be displayed from the CloudWatch console. Click on Metrics in the navigation pane on the left.

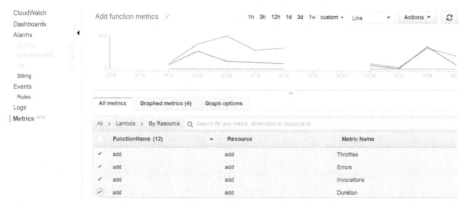

5. CloudWatch alarms can also be configured for the Lambda function metrics. Click on Alarms in the navigation pane on the left. Select a Lambda function metric by clicking on All Functions, Functions by Name, or By Resource.

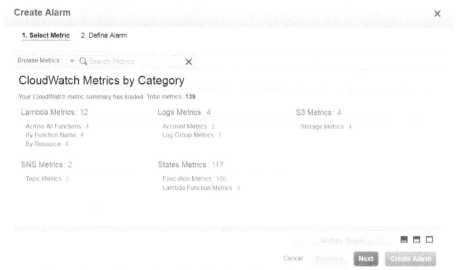

6. Enter the configuration of each alarm. Enter its name, description, duration and notification actions, and then click on Create Alarm.

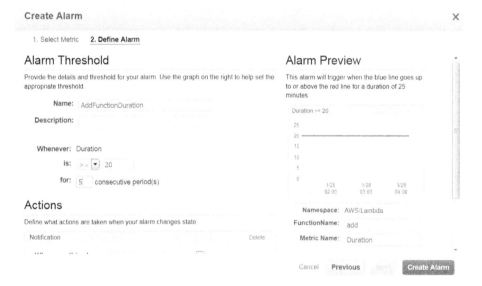

7. The alarm is displayed in the alarm summary menu. An alarm has three possible states:
   - OK - The metric is within the defined threshold.
   - ALARM - The metric is outside of the defined threshold.

- INSUFFICIENT_DATA - The alarm has just started, the metric is not available, or not enough data is available for the metric to determine the alarm state.

12.4 Deploying Lambda Functions

Lambda functions may be deployed using CloudFormation Service Application Model (SAM) templates which are described in detail in a later chapter. Use the following steps to deploy a Lambda function:

1. Click on the Action button and select the Export function option.

Export your function   ✕

Download a deployment package (your code and libraries), and/or an AWS Serverless Application Model (SAM) file that defines your function, its events sources, and permissions.

You or others you share this file with can use CloudFormation to deploy and manage a similar serverless application. Click here to learn how to deploy a serverless application with CloudFormation.

Close   Download AWS SAM file   Download deployment package

2. Click on Download AWS SAM file. An example of a SAM template is shown below.

```
AWSTemplateFormatVersion: '2010-09-09'
Transform: AWS::Serverless-2016-10-31
Resources:
  LambdaFunctionOverHttps:
    Type: AWS::Serverless::Function
    Properties:
      Handler: handler
      Runtime: runtime
      Policies: AmazonDynamoDBFullAccess
      Events:
        HttpPost:
          Type: Api
          Properties:
            Path: 'DynamoDBOperations/DynamoDBManager'
            Method: post
```

13 Lambda Function CLI

13.1 Introduction

The AWS Command Line Interface can be used to manage any AWS service as well as Lambda functions and Step Functions. The CLI provides an extensive suite of commands that can be used to configure and control each AWS service. The syntax for all AWS CLI commands is as follows:

```
aws <service> <action> [options and parameters]
```

The `help` keyword can be used to show details of each command. This can be used in three ways:

- `aws help` – to show all available service
- `aws <service> help` – to show all actions for a particular service
- `aws <service> <action> help` – to show all options for a given service action

For example,

```
$ aws lambda create-function help
```

Many commands include parameters which may be strings or numeric values. For example:

```
$ aws lambda list-functions --max-items 1
```

13.1.1 CLI Skeleton

Most AWS CLI commands support `--generate-cli-skeleton` and `--cli-input-json` parameters that can be used to store parameters in JSON and read them from a file instead of typing them at the command line.

Execute the CLI command with the `--generate-cli-skeleton` option to view the JSON skeleton. Direct the output of the CLI command to a file which can then be edited to tailor the parameters as needed.

Pass the edited JSON configuration to the `--cli-input-json` parameter in the CLI command using the `file://` prefix.

13.2 CLI Command Installation

The CLI commands can be installed on Linux, Mac and Windows.

13.2.1 Installing on Linux and Mac

The CLI requires Python and pip. Ensure that the Python version is 2.6.5 or greater, 2.7.x or greater or 3.4.x or greater. Run `python --version` to check the version. To install the AWS CLI run:

```
$ sudo pip install awscli
```

13.2.2 Installing on Windows

Perform the following steps to install on Windows:

1. Download the AWS CLI MSI installer from `http://aws.amazon.com/cli`.
2. Run the MSI installer
3. Run Powershell from the Start menu
4. Verify that the AWS CLI is working by typing `aws --version` in PowerShell.

13.3 CLI Credentials

Create the access key and the secret access using the IAM service in the AWS Management Console. To configure the AWS credentials for a CLI session use the `aws configure` command.

```
$ aws configure
AWS Access Key ID [*********************]:
AWS Secret Access Key [*********************]:
Default region name [us-west-1]: region
Default output format [None]:
```

The credentials are stored locally in the `.aws/credentials` file:

```
$ more .aws/credentials
[default]
aws_access_key_id = adminuser-access-key-id
aws_secret_access_key = adminuser-secret-access-key-id
```

13.4 Lambda Function CLI Summary

The AWS CLI Lambda functions CLI commands include:

- `add-permission`
- `create-alias`
- `create-event-source-mapping`
- `create-function`
- `delete-alias`
- `delete-event-source-mapping`
- `delete-function`
- `get-account-settings`

- `get-alias`
- `get-event-source-mapping`
- `get-function`
- `get-function-configuration`
- `get-policy`
- `invoke`
- `invoke-async`
- `list-aliases`
- `list-event-source-mappings`
- `list-functions`
- `list-versions-by-function`
- `publish-version`
- `remove-permission`
- `update-alias`
- `update-event-source-mapping`
- `update-function-code`
- `update-function-configuration`

To get details on the syntax and usage of the AWS Powershell commands use the `help` command.

13.5 Create a Lambda function

To create a Lambda function instance, use the `create-function` command.

```
$ aws lambda create-function
            --region region
            --function-name function-name
            --zip-file fileb://file-path/source-file.zip
            --role execution-role-arn
            --handler handler
            --runtime runtime
            --timeout timeout
            --memory-size size
            --description description
            --publish | --no-publish
            --vpc-config vpc-config
            --dead-letter-config dlc
            --environment environment
            --kms-key-arn key-arn
```

The deployment package is a zip or jar file of the source code.

The .zip file can optionally be uploaded to an Amazon S3 bucket in the same AWS region, and then the bucket and object name can be specified in the `create-function` command. The `--zip-file` parameter by the `--code` parameter, as shown below:

```
--code S3Bucket=bucket-name, S3Key=zip-file-object-key
```

13.6 Invoke a Lambda function

To invoke a Lambda function, use the `invoke` command.

```
$ aws lambda invoke --function-name hello outfile
{
   "StatusCode": 200
}
cat outfile
"Hola mundo"
```

The Lambda function can also be invoked with the `Event` invocation-type or the `DryRun` invocation type. `DryRun` is used to verify access to a function without running it.

```
aws lambda invoke --function-name hello --invocation-type Event
outfile
{
   "StatusCode": 202
}
aws lambda invoke --function-name hello --invocation-type DryRun
outfile
{
   "StatusCode": 204
}
```

If the `invoke` command includes a `--log-type` parameter set to `Tail` for an invocation-type parameter with value `RequestResponse`, the AWS Lambda returns the base64-encoded last 4 KB of log data produced by the Lambda function.

```
aws lambda invoke --function-name hello --log-type Tail outfile
{
   "LogResult": log-result,
   "StatusCode": 200
}
```

13.7 Update Lambda Function Configuration

To update Lambda function configuration, use the `update-function-configuration` command.

```
aws lambda update-function-configuration
   --function-name function-arn
   --region region
   --timeout timeout
   --profile adminuser
```

13.8 Add Lambda Function Permissions

To add Lambda function permissions, use the `add-permission` command.

```
aws lambda add-permission
  --function-name function-arn
  --region region
  --statement-id unique-id
  --action "lambda:InvokeFunction"
  --principal s3.amazonaws.com
  --source-arn arn:aws:s3:::source-bucket-name
  --source-account bucket-owner-account
  --profile adminuser
```

13.9 Update Lambda Function Code

During Lambda function development it is useful to be able to update the code for a Lambda function. This is done by creating a new zip file and then using the `update-function-code` CLI command.

```
zip -j lambda-function.zip lambda_function.py

aws lambda update-function-code
  --function-name function-arn
  --region region
  --zip-file fileb://lambda-function.zip
```

Alternatively, the Lambda function code can be updated from a deployment package in an S3 bucket.

```
aws lambda update-function-code
    --function-name function-arn
    --s3-bucket bucket-name
    --s3-key latest.zip
```

13.10 Create Event Source Mapping

To create an event source mapping from an event source, such as a DynamoDB stream or a Kinesis stream, to a Lambda function:

```
aws lambda create-event-source-mapping
    --region region
    --function-name lambda-function-name
    --event-source-arn event-source-arn
    --batch-size batch-size
    --enabled | --no-enabled
    --starting-position start-position
    --starting-position-timestamp timestamp
```

14 Lambda Function SDKs

AWS SDKs provide a set of language-specific function calls that can be invoked from your application. This allows for a close integration of AWS services, including Lambda and Step Functions, with the application logic. AWS provides Lambda Function SDKs for the following languages:

- Java
- .NET
- Node.js (Javascript)
- PHP
- Python
- Ruby
- Go

AWS Lambda functions also support SDKs for mobile devices such as iOS and Android.

14.1 Node.js

The AWS SDK for Node.js is installed using the npm package manager. To install, type the following into a terminal window:

```
npm install aws-sdk
```

A call to a Lambda function is shown below.

```
// import the AWS SDK
var AWS = require('aws-sdk');
var lambda = new AWS.Lambda({region: region,
                             apiVersion: '2015-03-31'});

var params = {
  FunctionName: function-name,
  ClientContext: context,
  InvocationType: invocation-type
};
  lambda.invoke(params, function(err, data) {
    if (err) console.log(err, err.stack); // an error occurred
    else    console.log(data);           // successful response
});
```

14.2 Python

The AWS SDK for Python is Boto3. This is a low-level client that represents AWS Lambda. A call to a Lambda function is shown below.

```
import boto3
```

```
lambda_client = boto3.client('lambda', region_name=region)

response = client.invoke(
    FunctionName=function-name,
    InvocationType=invocation-type,
    ClientContext=context
)
```

15 Serverless Application Model

CloudFormation provides a convenient way to specify, deploy, and configure serverless applications. A serverless application may be defined as a CloudFormation template and is deployed as a CloudFormation stack. A CloudFormation template is a declarative description of the cloud infrastructure and services.

Service Application Model (SAM) is an extension of AWS CloudFormation to define a common language to express the resources of serverless applications such as API Gateway, Lambda functions, Step Functions and DynamoDB.

15.1 CloudFormation Template

A CloudFormation Template (CFT) is formatted as JSON or YAML. A CloudFormation template consists of the following sections:

- `AWSTemplateFormatVersion`. The latest format version of `2010-09-09` and is currently the only valid value.
- `Description`. A description of what the template does.
- `Parameters`. This is a set of input parameters to customize a template.
- `Resource`. This specifies the resources that are to be deployed in a CloudFormation stack.
- `Transform`. This section indicates that SAM resources are declared in the template.
- `Mappings`. This section defines a mapping of keys and associated values for conditional parameters. A key may be matched to a corresponding value using the `Fn::FindInMap` intrinsic function in the `Resources` and `Outputs` section.
- `Conditions`. This section defines conditions that control whether certain resources are created or whether certain resource properties are assigned a value during stack creation or update.
- `Outputs`. This section specifies values that are returned from the template.

A CloudFormation template has the following structure.

```
AWSTemplateFormatVersion: '2010-09-09'
Description: 'CF template'
Transform: AWS::Serverless-2016-10-31
Parameters:
  parameters
Resources:
  resources
Mappings:
  mappings
Conditions:
```

```
    conditions
 Outputs:
    outputs
```

15.2 SAM Template

CloudFormation SAM templates must include a Transform section shown below. Lambda functions are defined in the Resources section of a SAM template. Any number of Lambda functions may be declared in the Resources section.

An example of a SAM template encoded as YAML for an S3 application is shown below. The template contains a Resource of type AWS::Serverless::Function that defines a Lambda function.

```
AWSTemplateFormatVersion: '2010-09-09'
Transform: AWS::Serverless-2016-10-31
Resources:
    function-name:
        Type: AWS::Serverless::Function
        Properties:
            Handler: handler
            Runtime: runtime
            CodeUri: s3://bucket-name/codepackage.zip
```

15.2.1 Lambda Function Resource

The Properties section for each Lambda function declaration in the template includes the following:

- The Handler attribute is the entry point in the Lambda function code where execution is started.
- The Runtime attribute specifies the programming environment for the Lambda function.
- The CodeUri attribute references the deployment package (zipfile or jar file) in an S3 bucket.
- Optionally, the Environment attribute defines environment variables that are passed to the Lambda function code and libraries
- Optionally, the Events sub-section defines the triggers for the Lambda function. Events.Type defines the type of event. Events.Properties includes various event-specific properties, such as S3 bucket or HTTP method.

15.2.2 SAM Template Examples

Several examples of SAM templates are shown below. An example of a SAM template for a Lambda function with S3 bucket ObjectCreated event trigger is shown below.

```
AWSTemplateFormatVersion: '2010-09-09'
Transform: AWS::Serverless-2016-10-31
Resources:
  TestFunction:
    Type: AWS::Serverless::Function
    Properties:
      Handler: index.handler
      Runtime: nodejs4.3
      Timeout: 60
      Policies: AWSLambdaExecute
      Events:
        Type: S3
        Properties:
          Bucket: !Ref SrcBucket
          Events: s3:ObjectCreated:*
  SrcBucket:
    Type: AWS::S3::Bucket
```

The SAM template for a Lambda function with an Amazon API Gateway trigger is shown below.

```
AWSTemplateFormatVersion: '2010-09-09'
Transform: AWS::Serverless-2016-10-31
Description: Outputs the time
Resources:
  TimeFunction:
    Type: AWS::Serverless::Function
    Properties:
      Handler: index.handler
      Runtime: nodejs4.3
      Events:
        TestApi:
          Type: Api
          Properties:
            Path: /TestResource
            Method: GET
```

15.2.3 Package and Deploy

Create a package using a CloudFormation template, such as the one shown above, which references artifacts, such as Lambda functions, in your local directory. The `package` command uploads the local artifacts specified by the `template-file` parameter to an S3 bucket and returns a copy of the template in the parameter `output-template-file`. This copy of the template has references to artifacts in the S3 bucket instead of references to local artifacts.

```
aws cloudformation package
        --region region
        --template-file template.yaml
        --s3-bucket s3-bucket-arn
```

```
--output-template-file packaged-template.yaml
```

Deploy the package with the `deploy` CLI command that uses the output template file. This will either create a new stack, or update an existing stack if its name is used.

```
aws cloudformation deploy --region region
                          --template-file packaged-template.yaml
                          --stack-name stack-name
                          --capabilities CAPABILITY_IAM
```

16 Lambda API Functions

This section includes a few examples of Lambda function API calls. For more detail see the AWS Lambda API Reference. This is a REST API that handles HTTP requests in the format:

```
POST /date/functions HTTP/1.1
```

These APIs include:

- AddPermission
- CreateAlias
- CreateEventSourceMapping
- CreateFunction
- DeleteAlias
- DeleteEventSourceMapping
- DeleteFunction
- GetAccountSettings
- GetAlias
- GetEventSourceMapping
- GetFunction
- GetFunctionConfiguration
- GetPolicy
- Invoke
- InvokeAsync
- ListAliases
- ListEventSourceMappings
- ListFunctions
- ListVersionsByFunction
- PublishVersion
- RemovePermission
- UpdateAlias
- UpdateEventSourceMapping
- UpdateFunctionCode
- UpdateFunctionConfiguration

16.1 Creating a Lambda Function

16.1.1 Create Request

Lambda function instances are created by invoking the following CreateFunction REST API request. The function metadata is created from the request parameters, and the code for the function is provided by a .zip file in the request body. If the function name already exists, the operation will fail. Note that the function name is case-sensitive. The syntax for the CreateFunction request is shown below.

```
POST /date/functions HTTP/1.1
Content-type: application/json
{
  "Code": {
    code-object,
  },
  "DeadLetterConfig": {
    "TargetArn": target-arn
  },
  "Description": user-description,
  "Environment": {
    "Variables": {
      attribute : value
    }
  },
  "FunctionName": function-name,
  "Handler": function-entry-point,
  "KMSKeyArn": "string",
  "MemorySize": memory-size,
  "Publish": publish-function,
  "Role": role-arn,
  "Runtime": runtime-identifier,
  "Timeout": timeout,
  "VpcConfig": {
    "SecurityGroupIds": [ security-group-ids ],
    "SubnetIds": [ subnet-id ]
  }
}
Payload
```

The body of the request has the following parameters.

- Code. The code for the Lambda function.
- DeadLetterConfig. The target ARN of a SQS queue or SNS topic.
- Description. Function description.
- Environment. The environment configuration settings.
- FunctionName. Function name.
- Handler. The function within the Lambda function code where execution is to begin.
- KMSKeyArn. The ARN of the KMS key used to encrypt the function's environment variables.
- MemorySize. The amount of memory, in MB, allocated to the Lambda function.
- Publish. If this Boolean parameter is true, AWS Lambda will create the Lambda function and also publish a version as an atomic operation.
- Role. The ARN of the IAM role that Lambda assumes to execute the Lambda function to access any other AWS resources.

- `Runtime`. The runtime environment for the Lambda function Valid Values: `nodejs | nodejs4.3 | java8 | python2.7 | dotnetcore1.0 |nodejs4.3-edge`
- `Timeout`. The function execution time at which Lambda should terminate the function. The default is 3 seconds.
- `VpcConfig`. If the Lambda function accesses resources in a VPC, this parameter identifies the list of security group IDs and subnet IDs. These must belong to the same VPC. At least one security group and one subnet ID must be provided.

16.1.2 Create Response

AWS Lambda sends an HTTP response:

```
HTTP/1.1 StatusCode
  X-Amz-Function-Error: FunctionError
  Payload
```

The response includes the following parameters:

- StatusCode. The `RequestResponse`, `Event` and `DryRun` invocation types have status codes of 200, 202 and 204 respectively.
- FunctionError. This has two values: `Handled` errors reported by the function, and `Unhandled` errors detected and reported by AWS Lambda.

16.2 Invoking a Lambda function

16.2.1 Invoke Request

Lambda functions are invoked using an HTTP POST request:

```
POST /date/functions/function-name/invocations?
                              Qualifier=qualifier
  HTTP/1.1
  X-Amz-Invocation-Type: invocation-type
  X-Amz-Log-Type: log-type
  X-Amz-Client-Context: client-context
  Payload
```

The Invoke request has the following parameters.

- ClientContext. Client-specific information passed to the Lambda function.
- FunctionName. The Lambda function name.
- InvocationType. `RequestResponse`, `Event`, or `DryRun` invocation type.
- LogType. If set to `Tail` in the request with the `InvocationType` of `RequestResponse`, AWS Lambda returns the base64-encoded last 4 KB of log data produced by your Lambda function in the `X-Amz-Logresult` header.

- Qualifier. To specify a Lambda function version or alias name. If a function version is specifed, the API uses the qualified function ARN to invoke a specific Lambda function. If an alias name is specified, the API uses the alias ARN to invoke the Lambda function version to which the alias points. If this parameter is not provided, then the API uses unqualified function ARN which results in invocation of the `$LATEST` version.
- Payload. Data in JSON format that is provided to the Lambda function as input.

16.2.2 Invoke Response

AWS Lambda sends an HTTP response:

```
HTTP/1.1 StatusCode
  X-Amz-Function-Error: FunctionError
  X-Amz-Log-Result: LogResult
  Payload
```

The response includes the following parameters:

- StatusCode. `RequestResponse`, `Event` and `DryRun` invocation types have status codes of 200, 202 and 204 respectively.
- FunctionError. This has two values: `Handled` errors reported by the function, and `Unhandled` errors detected and reported by AWS Lambda.
- LogResult. This is the base64-encoded logs for the Lambda function invocation. This is present only if the invocation type is `RequestResponse` and the logs were requested.
- Payload. This is the JSON response object from the Lambda function. This is present only if the invocation type is `RequestResponse`. For an error, the payload contains an error message. For the `Handled` errors the Lambda function will report this message. For `Unhandled` errors AWS Lambda reports the message.

17 Programming Models

17.1 Introduction

AWS Lambda functions currently support the following runtime environments:

- Javascript (Node.js)
- Python
- Java
- C#

The programming models for each language use the following in the Lambda function invocation:

- Handler specifies the entry point into the Lambda function.
- Event. AWS Lambda uses this parameter to pass in event data to the handler.
- Context. AWS Lambda uses the context parameter to provide the handler the runtime information of the Lambda function.

17.1.1 Handler

The handler of a Lambda function is its entry point of the language-specific code at which the execution starts. The handler is specified when the Lambda function is created. The handler signature differs for each runtime language.

17.1.2 Event Object

The Event object is used to pass data from the input event to the Lambda function. Java and C# support simple data types, POJOs, POCOs, and stream input/output.

17.1.3 Context Object

The Context object is used to pass information about the runtime environment to the handler. This provides methods and attributes to allow the Lambda function to retrieve the following information from the Lambda service:

- The time remaining until the Lambda function is terminated. The function `context.get_remaining_time_in_millis()` can be used to assess the progress of the Lambda function and if needed persist any data.
- `MemoryLimitInMB`. Memory limit, in MB, configured for the Lambda function.
- `FunctionName`. Name of the Lambda function that is running.
- `FunctionVersion`. The Lambda function version that is executing.

- InvokedFunctionArn. The function ARN or alias ARN used to invoke this function. An unqualified ARN executes the $LATEST version and aliases execute the function version it is pointing to.
- AwsRequestId. This is the AWS request ID associated with the request and is returned to the client that invoked this Lambda function. If AWS Lambda retries the function after an exception the request ID remains the same.
- LogStreamName. The CloudWatch log stream name for the particular Lambda function execution. It can be null if the IAM user provided does not have permission for CloudWatch actions.
- LogGroupName. The CloudWatch log group name associated with the Lambda function invoked. It can be null if the IAM user provided does not have permission for CloudWatch actions.
- ClientContext. Information about the client application and device when invoked through the AWS Mobile SDK. It can be null. Client context provides client information such as client ID, application title, version name, version code, and the application package name.
- The CloudWatch log group and log stream associated with the Lambda function.

Lambda function may contain logging statements which AWS Lambda writes to CloudWatch. If the Lambda function is invoked from the console, these logs are displayed on the console.

17.1.4 Deployment

For deployment Lambda function code is bundled with other artefacts such as libraries. For Node.js and Python the deployment package is a zip file that consists of the Lambda function code and any dependencies. For Java the deployment package is a zip file or a jar.

The deployment package is created automatically when the Lambda function code is written directly to the AWS Console, or it can be created manually. The sections on each runtime provide details about creating the deployment packages.

The deployment package may be uploaded directly or uploaded to an Amazon S3 bucket in the same AWS region as the Lambda function. The S3 bucket name and object key name are specified when creating the Lambda function using the AWS Management Console or the AWS CLI.

17.2 Javascript (Node.js) Lambda Functions

Amazon Lambda supports the Node.js runtime v4.3. Specify the runtime as nodejs4.3.

17.2.1 Handler

The following syntax is used for a Node.js handler function.

```
exports.handler = function(event, context, callback) {
  ...
  // Use callback() and return information to the caller.
}
```

Alternatively the following syntax can be used.

```
exports.handler = (event, context, callback) => {
  ...
  callback(null, 'Hello from Lambda');
}
```

The usage is as follows:

- `event`. AWS Lambda uses this parameter to pass in event data to the handler.
- `context`. AWS Lambda uses this parameter to provide the handler the runtime information of the Lambda function that is executing.
- `callback`. An optional callback to return information to the caller, otherwise return value is null.
- `handler`. The name of the function that AWS Lambda invokes. If the code is saved as `helloworld.js`, then handler is `helloworld.myHandler`.

If the invocation type is `RequestResponse`, AWS Lambda returns the result of the Node.js function call to the client invoking the Lambda function. If the handler does not return anything, AWS Lambda returns null. If the invocation type is `Event`, the value is discarded.

The callback may have the following formats:

- `callback();` - Indicates success but no information returned to the caller.
- `callback(null);` - Indicates success but no information returned to the caller.
- `callback(null, "success");` - Indicates success with information returned to the caller.
- `callback(error);` - Indicates error with error information returned to the caller.

A non-null value for the `error` parameter generates a handled exception.

The callback method automatically logs the string representation of non-null values of `error` to the Amazon CloudWatch Logs stream associated with the Lambda function. If the Lambda function was invoked synchronously (using the

`RequestResponse` invocation type), the callback returns a response body as follows:

- If `error` is null, the response body is set to the string representation of `result`.
- If the `error` is not null, the `error` value will be populated in the response body.

17.2.2 Deployment Package (Node.js)

For Node.js the deployment package is a zip file that consists of the Lambda function code and any dependencies. The deployment package is created automatically when the AWS console is used to create a Lambda function.

The deployment package can also be created manually. For example, if you want to create a deployment package that includes a Node.js code file which uses the `async` library.

1. Create a directory for the source code file and other library files.
2. Create the source code file in this directory.
3. Use npm to install the libraries used by your code. If your code uses the `async` library, use the following npm command.

```
npm install async
```

4. Your directory will then have the following structure:

```
filename.js
node_modules/async
node_modules/async/lib
node_modules/async/lib/async.js
node_modules/async/package.json
```

5. Zip the content of the folder to build the zip file deployment package.
6. Specify the .zip file name as the deployment package when the Lambda function is created.

To include your own binaries, including native ones, package them in the zip file. Reference the binaries using the relative path within the zip file. Include the following at the start of the Lambda function code:

```
process.env['PATH'] = process.env['PATH'] + ':' +
                      process.env['LAMBDA_TASK_ROOT']
```

17.3 Python Lambda Functions

17.3.1 Handler

The following syntax is used for a Python handler.

```
def handler-name(event, context):
    ...
    return return-value
```

The usage is as follows:

- `event`. To pass event data to the handler. This parameter may be one of the Python `dict`, `list`, `str`, `int`, `float`, or `NoneType` types.
- `context`. To provide runtime environment information to the handler, This is of `LambdaContext` type.
- The handler may optionally return a value. If the invocation type is `RequestResponse`, AWS Lambda returns the result of the Python function call to the client in the HTTP response to the invocation request, serialized into JSON. If the handler does not return anything, AWS Lambda returns null. If the invocation type is `Event`, the value is discarded.

For example,

```
def lambda_handler(event, context):
    name = event['name']
    address = event['address']
    return {
        'name' : 'Joe',
        'address': 'New York'
    }
```

17.3.2 Context Object

The context object provides the following methods:

- `get_remaining_time_in_millis()`. Returns the remaining execution time, in milliseconds, until AWS Lambda terminates the function.

The context object has the following attributes:

- `function_name`. Name of the Lambda function that is executing.
- `function_version`. The Lambda function version that is executing.
- invoked_function_arn. The function ARN or alias ARN used to invoke this function. An unqualified ARN executes the `$LATEST` version and aliases execute the function version it is pointing to.
- `memory_limit_in_mb`. Memory limit, in MB, configured for the Lambda function.

- `aws_request_id`. AWS request ID associated with the request. This is the ID returned to the client that called the `invoke` method. If AWS Lambda retries the invocation, the request ID remains unchanged.
- `log_group_name`. Name of the CloudWatch log group that contains logs written by the Lambda function.
- `log_stream_name`. Name of the CloudWatch log stream containing logs written by the Lambda function.
- `identity`. Information about the Amazon Cognito identity provider when invoked through the AWS Mobile SDK. It can be null.
- `identity.cognito_identity_id`
- `identity.cognito_identity_pool_id`
- `client_context`. Information about the client application and device when invoked through the AWS Mobile SDK. It can be null.
- `client_context.client.installation_id`
- `client_context.client.app_title`
- `client_context.client.app_version_name`
- `client_context.client.app_version_code`
- `client_context.client.app_package_name`
- `client_context.custom`. A `dict` of custom values set by the mobile client application.
- `client_context.env`. A `dict` of environment information provided by the AWS Mobile SDK

17.3.3 Exceptions

If the Python Lambda function raises an exception, AWS Lambda returns a stack trace in a JSON `stackTrace` array of stack trace items. For example, for a Lambda function that simply raises an exception:

```
def always_fail_handler(event, context):
    raise Exception('Failed!')
```

the following JSON is returned.

```
{
  "errorMessage": "Failed!",
  "stackTrace": [
    [
      "/var/task/lambda_function.py",
      3,
      "always_fail_handler",
      "raise Exception('Failed!')"
    ]
  ],
  "errorType": "Exception"
}
```

17.3.4 Logging

The following Python statements generate log entries:

- `print` statements.
- `Logger` functions in the `logging` module (for example, `logging.Logger.info` and `logging.Logger.error`.)

Both `print` and `logging.*` functions write logs to CloudWatch Logs but the `logging.*` functions write additional information to each log entry, such as time stamp and log level. For example, consider the following Python code example.

```
import logging
logger = logging.getLogger()
logger.setLevel(logging.INFO)

def my_logging_handler(event, context):
    logger.info('got event{}'.format(event))
    logger.error('Error condition')
```

If the Lambda function is invoked from the AWS Management console, the following Node.js statements will generate log entries:

- `console.log()`
- `console.error()`
- `console.warn()`
- `console.info()`

For example:

```
exports.myHandler = function(event, context, callback) {
    console.log("value1 = " + event.key1);
    console.log("value2 = " + event.key2);
    console.log('Received event:' JSON.stringify(event, null,
2));
    callback(null, "some success message");
}
```

17.3.5 Deployment Package

For Python, the deployment package is a zip file that consists of the Lambda function code and any dependencies. The deployment package is created automatically when the AWS console is used to create a Lambda function.

Use these steps to create a deployment package for a Python Lambda function manually.

1. Create a project directory for the code file and other library files.
2. Create the Python source files in this directory.
3. Install any libraries in this directory using `pip`.

```
pip install module-name -t /path/to/project-dir
```
For example, the following command installs the `requests` HTTP library.
```
pip install requests -t /path/to/project-dir
```

4. Zip the content of the project directory to create the deployment package.

AWS Lambda includes the AWS SDK for Python (Boto3), so it does not need to be included in the deployment package.

This is a brief introduction to creating the deployment package. See the AWS Lambda function documentation for complete details.

17.4 Java Lambda Functions

The syntax for a Java handler is as follows:

```
outputType handler-name(inputType input, Context context) {
   ...
}
```

The inputType and outputType can be one of the following:

*   Simple Java types such as `String`, `Integer`, `Boolean`.
*   POJO type. AWS Lambda will automatically serialize and deserialize input and output JSON based on the POJO type.
*   Predefined AWS event types defined in the `aws-lambda-java-events` library. For example `S3Event` is one of the POJOs predefined in the library that provides methods for you to easily read information from the incoming Amazon S3 event.

AWS Lambda provides the following Java libraries to process events:

*   `aws-lambda-java-core`. This library provides the Context object `RequestStreamHandler`, and the `RequestHandler` interfaces. The `Context` object provides runtime information about your Lambda function. The predefined interfaces provide one way of defining your Lambda function handler.
*   `aws-lambda-java-events`. Processing of predefined types to process events published by Amazon S3, Amazon Kinesis, Amazon SNS, and Amazon Cognito.
*   Custom Appender for Log4j 1.2. Use the custom Log4j appender provided by AWS Lambda for logging from Lambda functions.

17.4.1 Exceptions

If the Java Lambda function raises an exception, AWS Lambda returns a handled error with JSON stack trace as shown below.

```
{
  "errorMessage": "Failed",
  "errorType": "java.lang.Exception",
  "stackTrace": [
    "example.Hello.handler(Hello.java:9)",
    ...
  ]
}
```

17.4.2 Logging

Lambda function Java handlers may contain logging statements. AWS Lambda writes these logs to CloudWatch. The following Java statements can be used to write logs:

- Custom Appender for Log4j 1.2. AWS Lambda supports Log4j 1.2 by providing a custom appender. You can use the custom Log4j appender provided by Lambda for logging from your lambda functions. Every call to Log4j methods, such as `log.debug()` or `log.error()`, will result in a CloudWatch Logs event. The custom appender is called `LambdaAppender` and must be used in the `log4j.properties` file. You must include the `aws-lambda-java-log4j` artifact (`artifactId:aws-lambda-javalog4j`) in the deployment package (.jar file).
- `LambdaLogger.log()` Each call to `LambdaLogger.log()` results in a CloudWatch Logs event, provided the event size is within the allowed limits.
- `System.out()`
- `System.err()`

17.4.3 Deployment Package

Building a Java deployment package is outside the scope of the introduction. The descripion of building the Java deployment package can be found in the AWS Lambda function documentation.

17.5 C# Lambda Functions

17.5.1 Lambda function Handler

The C# handlers for Lambda functions as defined as instances or static methods in a class.

```
return-type handler-name(input-type input, ILambdaContext
context) {
  ...
}
```

The usage is as follows:

- `input`. The input parameter is the event data.
- `context`. An optional parameter is used access the Lambda context object.
- `return-type`. If the invocation type is `RequestResponse` (synchronous execution), AWS Lambda returns the result of the function call serialized into JSON. If the handler does not return anything, AWS Lambda returns null. If the invocation type is `Event` (asynchronous execution), the `return-type` should be `void`.

17.5.2 Context Object

The Lambda context object is accessed using a method parameter of type `ILambdaContext` which provides the following runtime information:

- `MemoryLimitInMB`. Memory limit, in MB, you configured for the Lambda function.
- `FunctionName`. Name of the Lambda function that is running.
- `FunctionVersion`. The Lambda function version that is executing.
- `InvokedFunctionArn`. The ARN used to invoke this function. It can be function ARN or alias ARN. An unqualified ARN executes the `$LATEST` version and aliases execute the function version it is pointing to.
- `AwsRequestId`. AWS request ID associated with the request. This is the ID returned to the client that invoked this Lambda function. You can use the request ID for any follow up enquiry with AWS support. Note that if AWS Lambda retries the function (for example, in a situation where the Lambda function processing Amazon Kinesis records throw an exception), the request ID remains the same.
- `LogStreamName`. The CloudWatch log stream name for the particular Lambda function execution. It can be null if the IAM user provided does not have permission for CloudWatch actions.
- `LogGroupName`. The CloudWatch log group name associated with the Lambda function invoked. It can be null if the IAM user provided does not have permission for CloudWatch actions.
- `ClientContext`. Information about the client application and device when invoked through the AWS Mobile SDK. It can be null. Client context provides client information such as client ID, application title, version name, version code, and the application package name.
- `Identity`. Information about the Amazon Cognito identity provider when invoked through the AWS Mobile SDK. It can be null.

- `RemainingTime`. Remaining execution time till the function will be terminated. At the time you create the Lambda function you set maximum time limit, at which time AWS Lambda will terminate the function execution. Information about the remaining time of function execution can be used to specify function behavior when nearing the timeout. This is a `TimeSpan` field.
- `Logger`. The Lambda logger associated with the ILambdaContext object

The following C# code snippet shows a handler function that displays the value of the input parameter and then prints some of the context information.

```
public async Task Handler(ILambdaContext context)
{
  Console.Writeline("Function name: " + context.FunctionName);
  Console.Writeline("RemainingTime: " + context.RemainingTime);
  await Task.Delay(TimeSpan.FromSeconds(0.42));
  Console.Writeline("RemainingTime after sleep: " +
      context.RemainingTime);
}
```

17.5.3 Deployment Package (C#)

Details of the C# deployment package can be found in the AWS Lambda function documentation.

18 AWS Tools for Windows PowerShell

The AWS PowerShell scripting environment can be used to manage AWS services.

Create the access key and the secret access using the IAM service in the AWS Management Console, then store the keys locally in the `.aws/credentials` file:

```
cat .aws\credentials
[default]
aws_access_key_id = adminuser access key ID
aws_secret_access_key = adminuser secret access key ID
```

To get details on the syntax and usage of the AWS Powershell commands use the `get-help` or the `help` command,

```
get-help invoke-LMFunction
NAME
  Invoke-LMFunction
SYNOPSIS
  Invokes the Invoke operation against Amazon Lambda.
SYNTAX
  Invoke-LMFunction [[-FunctionName] <System.String>]
  [[-Payload] <System.String>]
  [[-ClientContext] <System.String>]
  [[-InvocationType] <Amazon.Lambda.InvocationType>]
  [[-LogType] <Amazon.Lambda.LogType>]
  [-Force <System.Management.Automation.SwitchParameter>]
  [<CommonParameters>]
```

18.1 Lambda function Command-lets

The Powershell CLI has several command-lets that are used to manage Lambda functions. These can be listed using **get-command** with the −noun or −verb filters. For example:

```
get-command -noun *function*

CommandType       Name                                  ModuleName
-----------       ----                                  ----------
Cmdlet            Get-LMFunction                        AWSPowerShell
Cmdlet            Get-LMFunctionConfiguration           AWSPowerShell
Cmdlet            Get-LMFunctions                       AWSPowerShell
Cmdlet            Get-LMVersionsByFuncti                AWSPowerShell
Cmdlet            Invoke-LMFunction                     AWSPowerShell
Cmdlet            Invoke-LMFunctionAsync                AWSPowerShell
Cmdlet            Publish-LMFunction                    AWSPowerShell
Cmdlet            Remove-LMFunction                     AWSPowerShell
Cmdlet            Update-LMFunctionCode                 AWSPowerShell
Cmdlet            Update-LMFunctionConfiguration AWSPowerShell
```

As an example, to list all configured Lambda functions, use the `Get-LMFunctions` command.

```
Get-LMFunctions
CodeSha256    : uXE0eU+fdZQCE6YcgtRk3R0moP3rdPW5szcnzy9L9Uo=
CodeSize      : 236
Description   : hello world
Environment   :
FunctionArn   : arn:aws:lambda:region:account:function:hello
FunctionName  : hello
Handler       : lambda_function.lambda_handler
KMSKeyArn     :
LastModified  : 2016-11-29T21:13:14.171+0000
MemorySize    : 128
Role          : arn:aws:iam::account:role/lambda_basic_execution
Runtime       : python2.7
Timeout       : 3
Version       : $LATEST
VpcConfig     : Amazon.Lambda.Model.VpcConfigDetail
```

19 Step Functions

The Step Function service is an AWS compute service that allows you to orchestrate and manage workflows in the cloud. These workflows may be individual Lambda functions or custom activities executing in the cloud. Step Functions is a complementary service to AWS Lambda as it allows you to coordinate multiple Lambda functions to create a serverless application. Step Functions can be used to maintain state and execution order between the stateless Lambda functions.

The Step Function service provides a state machine infrastructure that allows individual Lambda functions and activities to be sequenced and coordinated for execution.

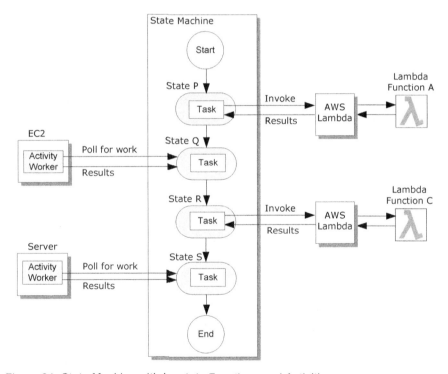

Figure 31: State Machine with Lambda Functions and Activities

Step Functions provide additional capabilities that can be used to create a serverless application:

• Lambda functions can in executed in sequential order.

- Lambda functions can in executed in parallel.
- Retry and catch constructs for tasks that invoke Lambda functions.
- Allow code to run for longer than the lifespan of a Lambda function.
- Audit logging for Lambda functions.

19.1 State Machines

Each state machine defines a set of states and the transitions between them. There are a number of different types of states that are summarized in the diagram below. States perform work, make decisions, and control progress through the state machine.

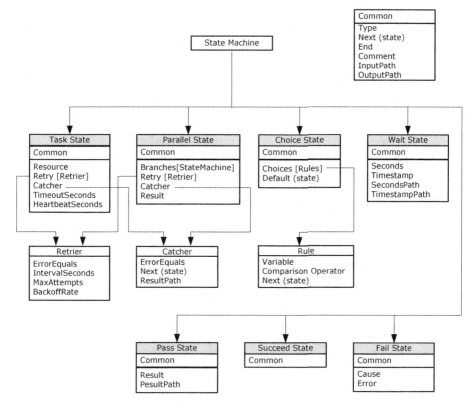

Figure 32: Step Function States

This diagram shows the different types of states as well as the various parameters that are used in each state. All states have a common set of parameters.

19.2 State Machine Definition

The State Machines are defined using JSON syntax using the Amazon States Language. An example of the JSON for a single state is shown below.

A state machine has the key elements:

1. Start state. This is the initial state of the state machine.

2. A list of states that comprise the state machine.

3. Each state has a name, a state type and a possible associated resource such as a Lambda function. The state types include:

   - Task
   - Pass
   - Parallel
   - Choice
   - Wait
   - Succeed
   - Fail

4. A transition to the next state, or an end of execution marker.

For example a Task state may include a Resource parameter that references a Lambda function as shown below in a snippet of the AWS States Language that is used to define Step Functions.

```
"States": {
  "HelloWorld": {
    "Type": "Task",
    "Resource":"arn:aws:lambda:region:account:function:function",
    "End": true
  }
}
```

Details of the AWS States Language are covered in section 22.

19.2.1 Executions

An execution is an executing instance of a state machine. A state machine can be have multiple, simultaneous executions. An execution is passed the JSON formatted input data and returns JSON formatted output data.

Once a state machine has been created, an execution can be started from the following:

- StartExecution API

- AWS Management Console
- `start-execution` CLI command
- Language-specific SDK call

An execution may be started, stopped and inspected using the following CLI commands:

- `describe-execution`
- `get-execution-history`
- `list-executions`
- `start-execution`
- `stop-execution`

19.2.2 Execution Events

Progress through a state machine execution is marked by events. Each event has a type, timestamp, and details related to the specific event type. These events can be viewed using the CLI command `get-execution-history` and are very useful for debugging the interactions between states, Lambda functions and activities.

Events that relate to overall execution operation include:

- ExecutionFailed
- ExecutionStarted
- ExecutionSucceeded
- ExecutionAborted
- ExecutionTimedOut

Events related to activities:

- ActivityFailed
- ActivityScheduleFailed
- ActivityScheduled
- ActivityStarted
- ActivitySucceeded
- ActivityTimedOut

State-specific events:

- ChoiceStateEntered
- ChoiceStateExited
- FailStateEntered
- SucceedStateEntered
- SucceedStateExited

- TaskStateEntered
- TaskStateExited
- PassStateEntered
- PassStateExited
- ParallelStateEntered
- ParallelStateExited
- WaitStateEntered
- WaitStateExited

Lambda function events:

- LambdaFunctionFailed
- LambdaFunctionScheduleFailed
- LambdaFunctionScheduled
- LambdaFunctionStartFailed
- LambdaFunctionStarted
- LambdaFunctionSucceeded
- LambdaFunctionTimedOut

19.3 State Machine Input and Output

State Machines are passed initial input data when an execution is started. This input data is in JSON format and is the `input` parameter of a start-execution CLI command.

```
aws --region=us-west-2 stepfunctions start-execution
    --state-machine-arn arn:aws:states:region:account:
                                    stateMachine:SM1
    --input file://input.json
```

JSON data is passed from one state to the next state as shown in Figure 31. The input data for the first state is the execution input data. The output data for each state must be in JSON format. Each state may either modify the input data that is receives from the previous state, or pass it on to the next state unchanged.

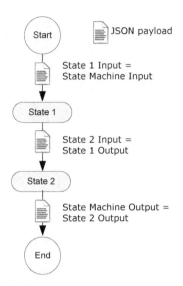

Figure 33: State Input and Output

JSON data is also passed to a Lambda function when it is invoked from a Task State. The JSON data is passed as the payload of the request sent to the Lambda function. If the Lambda function returns a response to the State Machine the response carries the JSON payload also.

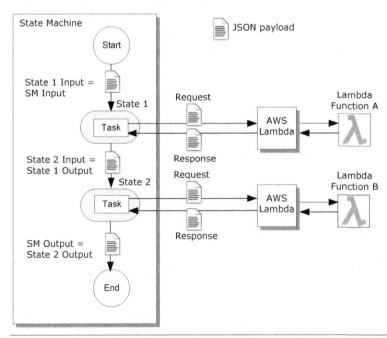

Figure 34: JSON Payload between State Machine and Lambda function

19.3.1 JSON Data Filters

The input JSON data structure for a state is passed through the processing logic of a state and is delivered as an output JSON data structure to the next state.

Three filters operate on the JSON data structures: `InputPath`, `ResultPath` and `OutputPath`:

1. `InputPath` selects the part of the JSON input that is used for task processing.

2. `ResultPath` selects the part of the result from the processing logic that is combined with the JSON input.

3. `OutputPath` selects the part that is sent as JSON output to the next state.

The JSON data filters used for a successful execution through a state machine which has one task state invoking a Lambda function are shown below.

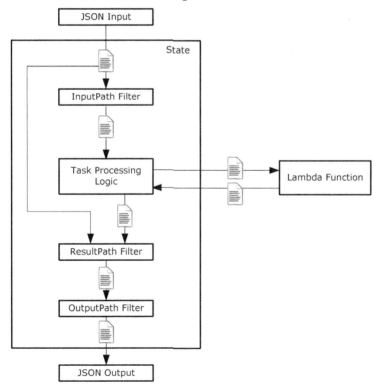

Figure 35: JSON Processing within a State

JSON Path Expressions

The values of these filters are JSON Path expressions. The JSON Path expression uses the symbol $ to represent the outer level JSON object.

The top level of an object in a JSON Path expression is referred to with the $ symbol, and its elements are accessed using dot (.) notation. Nested elements can be selected using further dots ($.x.y) to select sub-levels of the structure. For example, given this JSON data:

```
{
  "x": 123,
  "y": ["a", "b", "c"],
  "z": {
    "a": true,
    "b": 4
  }
}
```

The following table shows the values obtained by applying various JSON path expressions to the data:

Path	Value
$.x	123
$.y	["a", "b", "c"]
$.z.a	true

Payload Filters

The InputPath field selects a part of the JSON input to be passed to the state's processing logic. If this field is not specified, it defaults to $ which represents the whole JSON input. If this field is null, the input is discarded so the JSON input represents empty object {}.

A JSON path can select a subset of values. For example,

JSON input is {"a": [1, 2, 3, 4]}
InputPath JSON path is $.a[1..2]
Result will be: [2, 3]

The ResultPath field selects a part of the JSON input to be overwritten by, or added to, with result data from the state's processing logic. If the ResultPath is omitted, it defaults to $, which overwrites the entire input.

The OutputPath field selects the output from the ResultPath filter that is to be sent as JSON output data. If omitted, this defaults to $, which sends the whole of the ResultPath as JSON output.

19.4 Activities and Workers

State Machines perform tasks that are either Lambda functions or Activities. An Activity is performed by a worker that is hosted on any machine which has access to AWS Step Functions such as an EC2 instance, AWS container or Mobile device.

A task state can invoke an Activity by referencing its ARN using the Resource statement as shown below.

```
{
  "States": {
    "ActivityState": {
    "Type": "Task",
    "Resource":"arn:aws:states:region:account:
                              activity:function",
    "TimeoutSeconds": 300,
    "HeartbeatSeconds": 60,
    "End": true
    }
  }
}
```

Workers poll the State Machine to request for work. On receipt of the work, the worker performs the work and sends the response back to the State Machine.

This task state should include the TimeoutSeconds field to specify how long the state is to wait for polling requests from the worker. In addition, the state should include the HeartbeatSeconds field to specify the expected time between heartbeat requests received from the worker. If the activity does not receive a task request from the worker, a timeout is declared and the state terminates.

A worker must be structured as a polling loop to repeatedly invoke the activity task GetActivityTask to request for work. The state waits for this request from the activity worker. The state activity sends a response to the worker with the details of the task to be performed. The GetActivityTask call will return input data that is to be processed by the worker.

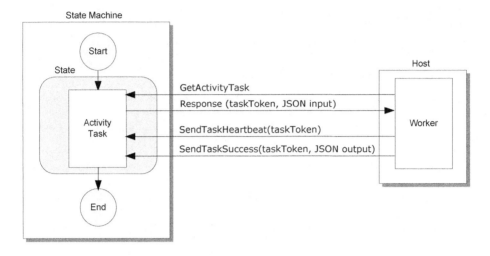

Figure 36: Step Function Activity Task

A worker is implemented in any language that can make AWS Step Functions API calls.

The worker reports the results, encoded as JSON, to the State Machine execution using the API calls SendTaskSuccess or SendTaskFailure. These calls must include a taskToken that was passed by GetActivityTask. The call SendTaskSuccess includes the worker's results in jsonOutput. The code snippet below shows a polling loop:

```
while (true) {
   [taskToken, jsonInput] = GetActivityTask();
   try {
      // Worker functionality
      ...
      SendTaskSuccess(taskToken, jsonOutput);
   } catch (Exception e) {
      SendTaskFailure(taskToken, reason, errorCode);
   }
}
```

A long-lived worker can also use the SendTaskHeartbeat to report to the State Machine activity that it is still active processing a work item.

20 Step Function Development

Step Functions may be created, tested, and deployed using the AWS Management Console. Step Functions provide a set of blueprints to help you in evaluation and development. Using the AWS Console, you can develop Step Functions and display the state machines in graphical form.

20.1 Development Stages

Step Function development includes the following steps:

1. Define Step Function state machines using JSON.

2. View the Step function state machines on the AWS Management console.

3. Initiate the execution of Step function state machines.

4. Monitor the execution of Step Functions.

20.2 Creating a State Machine

Use the AWS Step Function Console to create a State Machine as follows:

1. Click on the Create State Machine button on the Resource Groups dashboard.

2. The Create State Machine page is displayed. Select a blueprint from the list or where you can enter you own code in the Code pane

| Dashboard
Tasks

Dashboard   Create State Machine

Give a name to your state machine

Enter your name here

You can now create your own state machine with your own code or choose a blueprint below

Hello World   Wait State   Retry Failure   Parallel

Catch Failure   Choice State

3. When a blueprint such as Choice State is selected, a graphical view will be displayed in the Preview pane as well as the corresponding code in the Code pane.

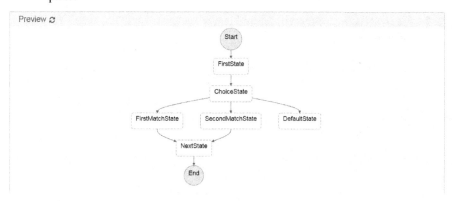

4. Click on the Create State Machine button below the Code pane. The IAM Role selection will be displayed. Select the StatesExecutionRole for the region.

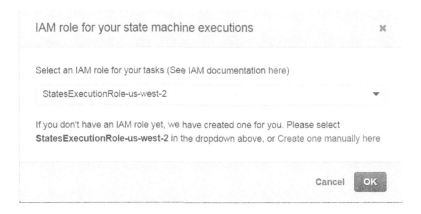

IAM role for your state machine executions   ✖

Select an IAM role for your tasks (See IAM documentation here)

StatesExecutionRole-us-west-2   ▼

If you don't have an IAM role yet, we have created one for you. Please select
StatesExecutionRole-us-west-2 in the dropdown above, or Create one manually here

Cancel   OK

20.3 Executing a State Machine

1. The state machine may now be executed by clicking on the New Execution button.

Services ˅   Resource Groups ˅   ✦

| Dashboard

Tasks

Dashboard : myChoiceStateMachine

myChoiceStateMachine

On this page you can add one or more executions for this state machine

✔ State machine successfully created
You can click the "New execution" button to start a new execution

New execution

2. Next, select the State Machine and start an Execution by clicking on the New Execution button.

| Dashboard

Tasks

Dashboard   myChoiceStateMachine

myChoiceStateMachine

On this page you can add one or more executions for this state machine

New execution   Stop execution   ↻   ❔

⊤ Search for executions

| Name | ▼ | Status | ▼ | Started | ▼ | End Time | ▼ |
No Executions

3. The New Execution Panel is displayed into which can be entered a block of JSON that is passed as input to the State Machine. Click on the Start Execution button below the JSON entry pane.

4. The state machine starts to execute. The Execution Details panel shows the status, input and output.

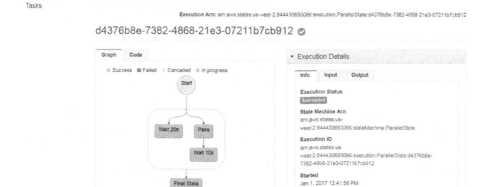

5. Each step of the execution is displayed in a panel below.

ID	Type	Timestamp
▸ 1	ExecutionStarted	Jan 1, 2017 12:41:58 PM
▸ 2	ParallelStateEntered	Jan 1, 2017 12:41:58 PM
▸ 3	WaitStateEntered	Jan 1, 2017 12:41:58 PM
▸ 4	PassStateEntered	Jan 1, 2017 12:41:58 PM
▸ 5	PassStateExited	Jan 1, 2017 12:41:58 PM
▸ 6	WaitStateEntered	Jan 1, 2017 12:41:58 PM
▸ 7	WaitStateExited	Jan 1, 2017 12:42:08 PM
▸ 8	WaitStateExited	Jan 1, 2017 12:42:18 PM
▸ 9	ParallelStateExited	Jan 1, 2017 12:42:18 PM
▸ 10	PassStateEntered	Jan 1, 2017 12:42:18 PM
▸ 11	PassStateExited	Jan 1, 2017 12:42:18 PM
▸ 12	ExecutionSucceeded	Jan 1, 2017 12:42:18 PM

20.4 Monitoring State Machine Executions

20.4.1 CloudWatch

State Machine execution metrics can be displayed from the AWS CloudWatch console. Click on Metrics in the navigation pane on the left.

Click on States below the All Metrics tab. Select Execution Metrics and then select the metrics to display.

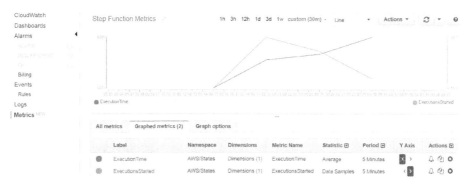

20.4.2 CloudTrail

AWS CloudTrail can be enabled to record Lambda function invocations as described previously. When CloudTrail logging is enabled, API calls made to specific Step Functions actions are also tracked in CloudTrail log files. The following actions are supported:

- CreateActivity
- CreateStateMachine

- DeleteActivity
- DeleteStateMachine
- StartExecution
- StopExecution

21 Amazon States Language

The Amazon States Language (ASL) defines the syntax for the state machines. This is a JSON Domain Specific Language that defines the states, their tasks and transitions between states. The JSON syntax may be validated using a StateLint which will be described in section 26.

Each state has a name, a state type and various optional fields. The state types include:

- Task
- Pass
- Parallel
- Choice
- Wait
- Succeed
- Fail

21.1 Common State Fields

There are a number of fields that are used by all states. These include:

- `Type` - he state type. This is a required field for all states.
- `Next` - Defines the transition to the next state to be executed. Some state types, such as Choice, have multiple transitions.
- `End` - Indicates that this state is a terminal state if set to true. There may be several terminal states in a state machine. Either the `Next` field or the `End` field can be used in a state but not both. Some state types, such as Choice, do not use the `End` field.
- `Comment` - Human-readable description of the state.
- `InputPath` - A path that selects the part of the state input to be used for state task processing. If omitted, the value $ indicates that the entire input is used.
- `OutputPath` - A path that selects the part of the state input to be passed to the state output. If omitted, the value $ indicates that the entire input is passed to the output.

21.2 Task State

A Task state is used to invoke a Lambda function or an Activity as shown below. The Task state has a `resource` field that contains the ARN of a Lambda function or an Activity that is to be executed.

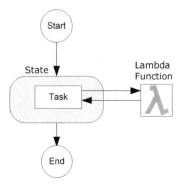

Figure 37: Task State

21.2.1 Task State with Lambda Function Resource

The JSON definition for a Task state that invokes a Lambda function is shown below.

```
{
  "Comment": "Hello World example.",
  "StartAt": "HelloWorld",
  "States": {
    "HelloWorld": {
      "Type": "Task",
      "Resource":"arn:aws:lambda:region:account:
                               function:function",
      "End": true
    }
  }
}
```

21.2.2 Task state with Activity Resource

The JSON definition for a Task state that has an Activity is shown below.

```
{
  "Comment": "Hello World example.",
  "StartAt": "HelloWorld",
  "States": {
    "HelloWorld": {
      "Type": "Task",
      "Resource":"arn:aws:states:region:account:
                               activity:function",
      "End": true
    }
  }
}
```

21.2.3 Task Retry on Failure

Step functions have a retry mechanism to handle task execution failures. A Task state has a `Retry` field to specify the retry logic when a specific error is returned from the execution of a resource. A `Retry` field has an array of Retrier objects, each of which defines a retry operation to be performed if a specific runtime error is detected.

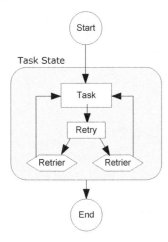

Figure 38: Task State Retry

Each Retrier has the following attributes:

- `ErrorEquals` - a non-empty array of Strings that match error names.
- `IntervalSeconds` - the interval between Retry attempts.
- `MaxAttempts` - the maximum number of retry attempts.
- `BackoffRate` - the multiplier by which the retry interval increases on each attempt.

The `ErrorsEquals` attribute is used to match the returned error name. Predefined errors begin with the prefix `States.`:

- `States.ALL`. This is a wild-card that matches any error name.
- `States.Timeout`. This is reported if task ran longer than the `TimeoutSeconds` value, or failed to send a heartbeat for a time longer than the `HeartbeatSeconds` value.
- `States.TaskFailed`. A task failed during the execution.
- `States.Permissions`. A task failed because it did not the privileges to execute the specified code.

Other user-defined error names may also be returned from the Lambda function.

An example of a JSON definition for a Retry is shown below. Several Retriers are defined in which the Lambda function is invoked again if it returns a `States.TaskFailed` error, a user-defined `LambdaError` error or the `States.ALL` error.

```
{
    "Comment": "Retry example",
    "StartAt": "HelloWorld",
    "States": {
     "HelloWorld": {
        "Type": "Task",
        "Resource": "arn:aws:lambda:region:account:
                                    function:function",
        "Retry": [
          {
            "ErrorEquals": ["LambdaError"],
            "IntervalSeconds": 1,
            "MaxAttempts": 2,
            "BackoffRate": 2.0
          },
          {
            "ErrorEquals": ["States.TaskFailed"],
            "IntervalSeconds": 30,
            "MaxAttempts": 2,
            "BackoffRate": 2.0
          },
          {
            "ErrorEquals": ["States.ALL"],
            "IntervalSeconds": 5,
            "MaxAttempts": 5,
            "BackoffRate": 2.0
          }
        ],
        "End": true
      }
    }
}
```

21.2.4 Task Retry on Timeout

Retry logic can be added to a state to retry a task if a `Timeout` error is returned from the execution resource. In the example below, the Lambda function is invoked two times if it returns a `Timeout` error.

```
{
    "StartAt": "State1",
    "States": {
      "State1": {
        "Type": "Task",
        "Resource": "arn:aws:lambda:region:account:
                                    function:function",
```

```
      "TimeoutSeconds": 2,
      "Retry": [
        {
          "ErrorEquals": ["States.Timeout"],
          "IntervalSeconds": 1,
          "MaxAttempts": 2,
          "BackoffRate": 2.0
        }
      ],
     "End": true
     }
  }
}
```

21.2.5 Catch with Alternate Actions on Failure

Catch logic can be added to a Task state to detect States.Timeout and States.ALL errors returned from a Lambda function and transition to other states. The Catch field includes ErrorEquals and Next fields that match on errors returned from a Lambda function and specify the next states respectively.

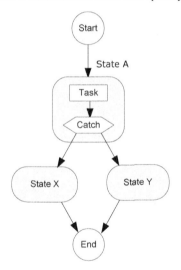

Figure 39: Catch with transitions to alternate states

```
{
  "States": {
    "State1": {
    "Type": "Task",
    "Resource": "arn:aws:lambda:region:account:function:function",
    "TimeoutSeconds": 2,
    "Catch": [
      {
        "ErrorEquals": ["States.Timeout"],
        "Next": "StateX"
```

```
    },
    {
      "ErrorEquals": ["States.ALL"],
      "Next": "StateY"
    }
  ],
  "End": true
  },
  "StateX": {
    "Type": "Pass",
    "Result": "Timeout detected",
    "End": true
  }
  "StateY": {
    "Type": "Pass",
    "Result": "Error detected",
    "End": true
  }
  }
  }
}
```

21.2.6 Catch with Alternate Actions on Timeout

Catch logic can be added to a state to catch a States.Timeout error returned from the execution resource and then transition to another state.

```
{
  "States": {
    "State1": {
      "Type": "Task",
      "Resource": "arn:aws:lambda:region:account:
                                    function:function",
      "TimeoutSeconds": 2,
      "Catch": [
        {
          "ErrorEquals": ["States.Timeout"],
          "Next": "StateX"
        }
      ],
      "End": true
    },
    "StateX": {
      "Type": "Pass",
      "Result": "Timeout detected",
      "End": true
    }
  }
}
```

21.3 Sequenced States

States can be coordinated to execute in sequential order with a transition defined from one state to the next state. A transition from one state to the next is specified using the `Next:` statement which references the next state to be executed on completion of the current state.

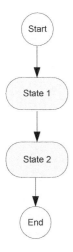

Figure 40: Sequenced States

The JSON for the sequenced states is shown below:

```
{
  "Comment": "Sequence of two states.",
  "StartAt": "State1",
  "States": {
    "State1": {
      "Type": "Task",
      "Resource":"arn:aws:lambda:region:account:
                              function:function1",
      "Next": "State2"
    },
    "State2": {
      "Type": "Task",
      "Resource":"arn:aws:lambda:region:account:
                              function:function2",
      "End": "true"
    },
  }
}
```

21.4 Parallel State

A number of states can be coordinated to execute in parallel. This allows the state machine to fork and join other states so they execute concurrently. Step Functions will make sure that all parallel state machines run to completion before transitioning to the next state, or terminating the state machine.

A parallel state is defined by a state type `Parallel` and includes an array of parallel `Branches`, each of which has separate states. Each branch receives a copy of the Parallel state's input data.

The parallel state generates an output array in which each element is the output for a branch. The elements of the output array need not be of the same type. The output array can also be inserted into the input data by using a `ResultPath` field.

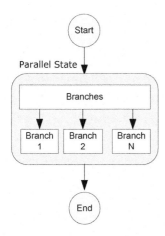

Figure 41: Step Function Parallel State Machines

The JSON for parallel states is shown below:

```
"ParallelState": {
  "Type": "Parallel",
  "Branches": [{
    "StartAt": "State1",
    "States": {
      "State1": {
        "Type": "Task",
        "Resource":"arn:aws:lambda:region:account:
                                    function:function1",
        "End": true
      }
    }
  },
  {
  "StartAt": "State2",
  "States": {
    "State2": {
      "Type": "Task",
```

```
        "Resource":"arn:aws:lambda:region:account:
                                    function:function2",
        "End": true
      }
    }
  }]
],
```

21.5 Choice State

A `Choice` state is used to select the next state based on a match on specific JSON payload value. The Choices are an array of matching conditions. Each match entry in the `Choices` array consists of:

- `Variable` - specifies the variable in the JSON payload that is to be matched.
- Matching condition. This includes `NumericEquals`, `StringEquals`.
- `Next` - This is the next state to be executed if there is a match for the specified condition.

There is also a `Default` field to handle unmatched values.

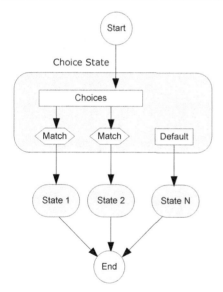

Figure 42: Step Function Choice State

A Choice state with matches on two values of variable $.foo in the JSON payload is shown below:

```
"ChoiceState": {
```

```
    "Type": "Choice",
    "Choices": [
      {
        "Variable": "$.foo",
        "NumericEquals": 1,
        "Next": "StateX"
      },
      {
        "Variable": "$.foo",
        "NumericEquals": 2,
        "Next": "StateY"
      }
    ],
    "Default": "DefaultState"
},
```

This Choice state would be followed by the following states.

```
"StateX": {
  "Type": "Task",
  "Resource": "arn:aws:lambda:region:account:function:functionX",
  "Next": "NextState"
},
"StateY": {
  "Type": "Task",
  "Resource": "arn:aws:lambda:region:account:function:functionY",
  "Next": "NextState"
},
"DefaultState": {
  "Type": "Fail",
  "Cause": "No Matches"
},
"NextState": {
  "Type": "Task",
  "Resource": "arn:aws:lambda:region:account:function:functionZ",
  "End": true
}
```

21.6 Wait State

A Wait state will wait for a number of seconds or until a specified timestamp value has occurred. A wait state has the following parameters:

- Seconds - The time, in seconds, to wait before transitioning to the state specified in the Next field.

- Timestamp - The absolute time to wait before transitioning to the state specified in the Next field. The time string must be in the RFC3339 profile of ISO 8601. In addition an uppercase "T" must separate the date and time parts. An uppercase "Z" must be used if there is no numeric time zone offset present, for example, "2017-01-17T14:45:00Z".

- `SecondsPath` - A time, in seconds, to wait before transitioning to the state specified in the `Next` field. The time value is obtained from the input data using the specified path.

- `TimestampPath` - An absolute time to wait until before transitioning to the state specified in the `Next` field. The timestamp value is obtained from the input data using the specified path.

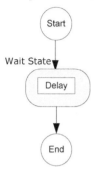

Figure 43: Wait State

An example of a JSON definition for a Wait state with a `Seconds` parameter is shown below:

```
{
  "WaitState": {
    "Type": "Wait",
    "Seconds": "30",
    "Next": "State1"
  }
}
```

An example of a JSON definition for a Wait state with a `TimestampPath` parameter is shown below. The `TimestampPath` uses a value from the JSON input.

```
{
  "WaitState": {
    "Type": "Wait",
    "TimestampPath": "$.StartTime",
    "Next": "State5"
  }
}
```

21.7 Pass State

A Pass state passes its input to its output without performing any task. This state may be used for debugging state machines.

In addition to the common state fields, Pass states allow the following fields:

- `Result` - Treated as the output of a virtual task to be passed on to the next state, and filtered as prescribed by the `ResultPath` field (if present).
- `ResultPath` - Specifies where (in the input) to place the "output" of the virtual task specified in `Result`.
- `OutputPath` - The input is further filtered as prescribed by the `OutputPath` field (if present) before being used as the state's output.

An example of the JSON definition of a Pass state is shown below:

```
"PassState": {
  "Type": "Pass",
  "Result": {
    "x": 130,
    "y": 349
  },
  "ResultPath": "$.coords",
  "Next": "End"
}
```

21.8 Succeed State

A Succeed state will stop an execution successfully. A Succeed state may be used to terminate a branch in a Choice state. A Succeed state has no `Next` or `End` field since it is a terminal state.
An example of the JSON definition of a Succeed state is shown below:

```
"SuccessState": {
  "Type": "Succeed"
}
```

21.9 State Machine Example

This is an example of a Step Function state machine that orchestrates the execution of several Lambda functions. It performs the following steps:

1. The `GetDataState` Task calls a Lambda function FN1 to retrieve data.
2. The `ValidationState` is a Choice state which validates the source data format. If invalid the state machine transitions to the Fail state `InvalidDataState`.
3. If valid it transitions to the Task state `SaveDataState` and calls a Lambda function FN2 to do some initial processing on the data.
4. The parallel processing state has two branches which allow the concurrent execution of Lambda function FN5 with Lambda functions FN3 and FN4.
5. Branch 1 has two Task states, `Branch1Start` and `Branch1End`, which call Lambda functions FN3 and FN4 and then terminate the state machine.

6. Branch 2 has one Task state `Branch2Start` that calls Lambda function FN5 and then terminates the state machine.

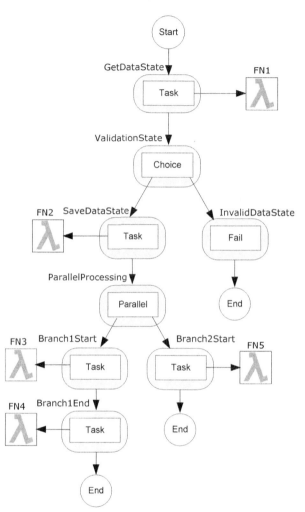

Figure 44: State Machine Example

```
{
  "Comment": "Orchestration of five Lambda functions",
  "StartAt": "GetDataState",
  "States": {
    "GetDataState": {
      "Type": "Task",
      "Resource": "Lambda_FN1",
      "Next": "ValidationState"
    },
```

```json
"ValidationState": {
  "Type": "Choice",
  "Choices": [
    {
    "Or": [
      {
        "Variable": "$.format",
        "StringEquals": "MP4"
      },
      {
        "Variable": "$.format",
        "StringEquals": "AVI"
      }
    ],
    "Next": "SaveDataState"
  }
  ],
  "Default": "InvalidDataState"
},
"SaveDataState": {
  "Type": "Task",
  "Resource": "Lambda_FN2",
  "Next": "ParallelProcessing"
},
"InvalidDataState": {
  "Type": "Fail",
  "Cause": "Data format not supported!",
  "Error": "InvalidDataFormat"
},
"ParallelProcessing": {
  "Type": "Parallel",
  "Branches": [
  {
    "StartAt": "Branch1Start",
    "States": {
      "Branch1Start": {
        "Type": "Task",
        "Resource": "Lambda_FN3",
        "Next": "Branch1End"
      },
      "Branch1End": {
        "Type": "Task",
        "Resource": "Lambda_FN4",
        "End": true
      }
    }
  },
  {
    "StartAt": "Branch2Start",
    "States": {
      "Branch2Start": {
        "Type": "Task",
        "Resource": "Lambda_FN5",
```

```
              "End": true
            }
          }
        }
      ],
      "End": true
      }
    }
}
```

22 Step Function Integrations

This chapter deals with how Step functions are integrated with various AWS services.

As described previously Step Function Activities can be hosted on AWS EC2 or ECS. These Activities can do long polling of Step Functions to request work from the Step Function, perform the work and then return the result to the Step function.

22.1 CloudWatch Events

CloudWatch Events (CWE) may also be used to execute a Step Functions state machine. A CloudWatch rule can be created to specify the schedule expression and the ARN of the Step function.

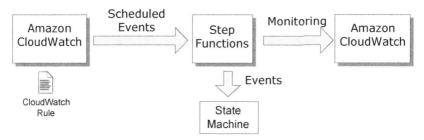

Figure 45: Step Function state machine scheduled from CloudWatch

22.1.1 Trigger Configuration

A CloudWatch rule to schedule a Step Function is configured using the AWS Management Console or by using CloudWatch CLI commands. The scheduling can be done using `rate` or `cron` expressions as described in section 8.9.

Click on CloudWatch in the AWS Management Console and select Events and Rules. Next, set the Event selector to Schedule and choose either a fixed duration or a Cron expression. Finally, select Step Functions state machine as the Target and enter the state machine name.

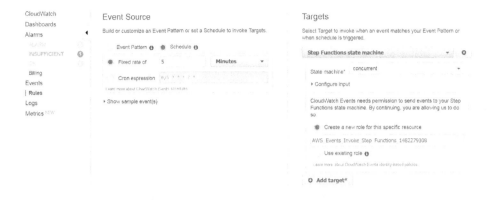

Use the CloudWatch CLI command `put-rule` to configure a scheduled event.

```
aws events put-rule --name rule-name
                    --schedule-expression 'rate(X minutes)'
```

The CloudWatch CLI command `put-targets` adds the Step function to this rule:

```
aws events put-targets --rule rule-name
                       --targets file://targets.json
```

The JSON file `targets.json` specifies a Step Function state machine as the target.

```
[{
  "Id": "1",
  "Arn": "arn:aws:states:region:account:
                  stateMachine:state-machine-name"
}]
```

22.2 CloudFormation

A CloudFormation resource may be used to create an AWS Step Function state machine.

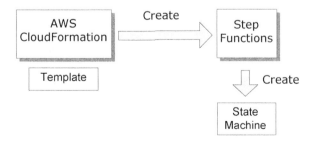

Figure 46: State Machine created from CloudFormation template

22.2.1 CloudFormation Template

A resource of type `AWS::StepFunctions::StateMachine` in the CloudFormation template is used to create a state machine as shown below. `DefinitionString` contains the Amazon States Language definition of the state machine and `RoleArn` is the ARN of the IAM role to use for the state machine.

```
AWSTemplateFormatVersion: '2010-09-09'
Description: description
Resources:
    statemachine-name:
        Type: AWS::StepFunctions::StateMachine
        Properties:
            DefinitionString: statemachine-definition
            RoleArn: statemachine-role-arn
```

CloudFormation automatically generates a name for the state machine. If the contents of the `DefinitionString` or `RoleArn` properties are changed and the stack is updated, then CloudFormation will generate a new state machine name and delete the old state machine.

22.2.2 Deploy CloudFormation Stack

Create a package using the CloudFormation `package` CLI command as described in section 2.4.5.

```
aws cloudformation package
        --region region
        --template-file template.yaml
        --s3-bucket s3-bucket-arn
        --output-template-file packaged-template.yaml
```

Deploy the package using the `deploy` CLI command.

```
aws cloudformation deploy --region region
                    --template-file packaged-template.yaml
                    --stack-name stack-name
                    --capabilities CAPABILITY_IAM
```

22.3 API Gateway

The integration of API Gateway and Step Function state machines can be used to create a wide variety of Web applications. Step functions can be invoked when the API Gateway service receives various different HTTP requests operations such as GET or POST methods to a registered URI for a HTTP endpoint.

Figure 47: Integration of API Gateway with Step Functions

The integration can be done in a similar manner to that described for Lambda functions in section 8.7.

22.3.1 Integration Configuration

When you create a method for the new API from the AWS Console you can specify the integration with a Step Function as shown below. Select Step Functions as the AWS Service and enter `StartExecution` as the Action. You can also use other actions such as `SendTaskSuccess` or `SendTaskFailure`.

To test the API Gateway to Step Function integration, use this `curl` command.

```
curl -X POST -d '{"input": "{}","name": "MyExecution",
    "stateMachineArn":
    "arn:aws:states:region:account:stateMachine:HelloWorld"}'
https://a1b2c3d4e5.execute-api.region.amazonaws.com/alpha/execution
```

23 Step Function CLI

State Machines may also be managed using the AWS CLI which can be downloaded and installed as described in section 13.2.

The AWS CLI offers a set of commands to create and manage Step Function state machines, activities and executions:

- `create-activity`
- `create-state-machine`
- `delete-activity`
- `delete-state-machine`
- `describe-activity`
- `describe-execution`
- `describe-state-machine`
- `get-activity-task`
- `get-execution-history`
- `help`
- `list-activities`
- `list-executions`
- `list-state-machines`
- `send-task-failure`
- `send-task-heartbeat`
- `send-task-success`
- `start-execution`
- `stop-execution`

Details about each command can be obtained by typing

```
aws stepfunctions <command-name> help
```

Other useful CLI commands include:

```
aws iam list-roles
```

23.1 list-state-machines

The `list-state-machines` CLI command lists existing state machines. Each entry in the list includes the creation date, ARN and name of the state machine. For example:

```
aws stepfunctions list-state-machines
{
    "stateMachines": [
        {
            "creationDate": 1483303312.652,
```

```
        "stateMachineArn": "arn:aws:states:region:account:
                            stateMachine:ParallelState",
        "name": "ParallelState"
    }
  ]
}
```

23.2 create-state-machine

The `create-state-machine` CLI command creates a state machine.

```
create-state-machine --name <value>
                     --definition <value>
                     --role-arn <value>
```

An example is shown below. Note the use of the back-slash to escape the quote characters in the `definition` parameter.

```
aws --region=us-west-2 stepfunctions create-state-machine
    --name foo
    --definition "{\"StartAt\":\"foo\",\"States\":{
                  \"foo\":{\"Type\":\"Pass\",\"End\":true}}}"
    --role-arn arn:aws:iam::account:
               role/service-role/StatesExecutionRole-region
{
    "creationDate": 1483411710.349,
    "stateMachineArn": "arn:aws:states:region:account:
                        stateMachine:foo"
}
```

Alternatively the States Language definition can be placed in a file and referenced using the `file://path-to-json-file` notation.

```
aws stepfunctions create-state-machine --name foo
        --definition file://hello.smspec --role-arn
    arn:aws:iam::account:role/service-role/StatesExecutionRole-
region
{
    "creationDate": 1483477773.061,
    "stateMachineArn": "arn:aws:states:region:account:
                                 stateMachine:foo"
}
```

The definition file has the JSON content:

```
{
   "StartAt":"foo",
   "States":{
     "foo":{
       "Type":"Pass",
       "End":true
     }
   }
```

}

23.3 delete-state-machine

The `delete-state-machine` CLI command deletes a state machine.

23.4 describe-state-machine

The `describe-state-machine` CLI command shows the details of a state machine. Note the use of `\"` to escape the double-quote in the state machine `definition` field in the example shown below.

```
aws stepfunctions describe-state-machine
    --state-machine-arn arn:aws:states:region:account:
                                        stateMachine:foo
{
    "status": "ACTIVE",
    "definition": "{\"StartAt\":\"foo\",\"States\":
                {\"foo\":{\"Type\":\"Pass\",\"End\":true}}}",
    "name": "foo",
    "roleArn": "arn:aws:iam::account:role/service-role/
                StatesExecutionRole-region",
    "stateMachineArn":
                "arn:aws:states:region:account:stateMachine:foo",
    "creationDate": 1483411710.349
}
```

The `describe-state-machine` CLI command shows the details of a state machine.

```
aws stepfunctions describe-state-machine
        --state-machine-arn
arn:aws:states:region:account:stateMachine:foo4
{
    "status": "ACTIVE",
    "definition":
     "{
      \"StartAt\":\"foo\",
        \"States\":{
          \"foo\":{
            \"Type\":\"Task\",
              \"Resource\":\"arn:aws:lambda:region:account:
                                        function:add\",
              \"End\":true}}}",
    "name": "foo4",
    "roleArn":"arn:aws:iam::account:
                role/service-role/StatesExecutionRole-region",
"stateMachineArn":"arn:aws:states:region:account:stateMachine:foo4,
    "creationDate": 1484870772.312
    }
```

23.5 list-executions

The `list-executions` CLI command lists the executions for a given state machine.

```
aws stepfunctions list-executions
    --state-machine-arn
            arn:aws:states:region:account:stateMachine:foo
{
  "executions": [
    {
      "status": "SUCCEEDED",
      "startDate": 1483412904.017,
      "name": "922acb2d-e138-4044-981d-3431b5e46d6e",
      "executionArn": "arn:aws:states:region:account:
        execution:foo:922acb2d-e138-4044-981d-3431b5e46d6e",
      "stateMachineArn": "arn:aws:states:region:account:
                                        stateMachine:foo",
      "stopDate": 1483412904.048
    }
  ]
}
```

23.6 start-execution

The `start-execution` CLI command starts an execution for a given state machine. The input data for an execution is passed using the input parameter. A file containing the input data in JSON format is referenced using the `file://`*path-to-json-file* notation.

```
aws stepfunctions start-execution
    --state-machine-arn arn:aws:states:region:account:
                        stateMachine:statemachine-name
    --input file://input.json
```

23.7 stop-execution

The `stop-execution` CLI command stops an execution for a given state machine.

```
aws stepfunctions stop-execution
    --state-machine-arn arn:aws:states:region:account:
                        stateMachine:statemachine-name
```

23.8 describe-execution

The `describe-execution` CLI command shows details for an execution.

```
aws stepfunctions describe-execution
    --execution-arn arn:aws:states:region:account:
                    execution:foo:execution-arn
{
```

```
  "status": "SUCCEEDED",
  "startDate": 1483412904.017,
  "name": "922acb2d-e138-4044-981d-3431b5e46d6e",
  "executionArn": "arn:aws:states:region:account:
                   execution:foo:execution-arn",
  "stateMachineArn": "arn:aws:states:region:account:
                                      stateMachine:foo",
  "stopDate": 1483412904.048,
  "output": "{}",
  "input": "{}"
}
```

23.9 describe-execution-history

The describe-execution-history CLI command shows the event details for an execution. The example below shows the successful execution through a state machine that has one task state that invokes a Lambda function. The following events are generated:

1. ExecutionStarted
2. TaskStateEntered
3. LambdaFunctionScheduled
4. LambdaFunctionStarted
5. LambdaFunctionSucceeded
6. TaskStateExited
7. ExecutionSucceeded

These state machine execution events are shown below.

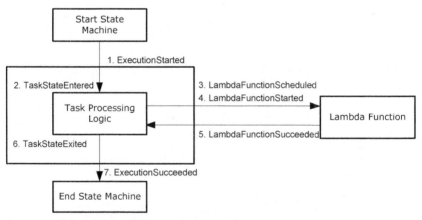

Figure 48: State Machine Execution Events

```
aws stepfunctions get-execution-history
    --execution-arn arn:aws:states:region:account:
                  execution:lambda-function:execution-arn
```

```json
{
  "events": [
    {
      "timestamp": 1484950187.764,
      "executionStartedEventDetails": {
        "input": {} ",
        "roleArn":"arn:aws:iam::account:role/service-role/
                  StatesExecutionRole-region"
      },
      "type": "ExecutionStarted",
      "id": 1,
      "previousEventId": 0
    },
    {
      "timestamp": 1484950187.8,
      "type": "TaskStateEntered",
      "id": 2,
      "stateEnteredEventDetails": {
        "input": "{}",
        "name": "state1"
      },
      "previousEventId": 0
    },
    {
      "timestamp": 1484950187.8,
      "lambdaFunctionScheduledEventDetails": {
        "input":{}",
        "resource":  "arn:aws:lambda:region:account:
                    function:lambda-function"
      },
      "type": "LambdaFunctionScheduled",
      "id": 3,
      "previousEventId": 2
    },
    {
      "timestamp": 1484950187.941,
      "type": "LambdaFunctionStarted",
      "id": 4,
      "previousEventId": 3
    },
    {
      "lambdaFunctionSucceededEventDetails": {
        "output": "{}"
      },
      "timestamp": 1484950188.024,
      "type": "LambdaFunctionSucceeded",
      "id": 5,
      "previousEventId": 4
    },
    {
      "timestamp": 1484950188.024,
      "stateExitedEventDetails": {
        "output": "{}",
```

```
        "name": "state1"
      },
      "type": "TaskStateExited",
      "id": 6,
      "previousEventId": 5
    },
    {
      "executionSucceededEventDetails": {
        "output": "{}"
      },
      "timestamp": 1484950188.024,
      "type": "ExecutionSucceeded",
      "id": 7,
      "previousEventId": 6
    }
  ]
}
```

23.10 create-activity

The `create-activity` CLI command creates an activity. Activities operate in concert with workers which are hosted on EC2 instances, AWS containers or mobile devices.

```
aws stepfunctions create-activity --name activity1
{
   "creationDate": 1483415802.344,
   "activityArn":
          "arn:aws:states:us-west-2:account:activity:activity1"
}
```

23.11 list-activities

The `list-activities` CLI command lists activities.

```
aws stepfunctions list-activities
{
  "activities": [
    {
      "creationDate": 1483415802.344,
      "name": "activity1",
      "activityArn": "arn:aws:states:region:account:
                                 activity:activity1"
    }
  ]
}
```

If there are no activities an empty list is returned.

```
aws stepfunctions list-activities
{
    "activities": []
}
```

23.12 describe-activity

The describe-activity CLI command describes an activity.

```
aws stepfunctions describe-activity --activity-arn
            arn:aws:states:region:account:activity:activity1
{
   "creationDate": 1483415802.344,
   "name": "activity1",
   "activityArn": "arn:aws:states:region:account:
                              activity:activity1"
}
```

23.13 delete-activity

The delete-activities CLI command deletes an activity.

```
aws stepfunctions delete-activity
   --activity-arn arn:aws:states:region:account:
                              activity:activity1
```

23.14 get-activity-task

A worker invokes the get-activity-task CLI command to poll the executing state machine to get a task scheduled for execution. This function informs the Step Function of the existence of an activity and returns an identifier for use in a state machine and when polling from the activity. The worker uses the send-task* calls to update the execution of its status.

```
aws get-activity-task --activity-arn activity-arn
   [--worker-name worker-name]
```

23.15 send-task-success

A worker invokes send-task-success to report that the task identified by the taskToken completed successfully.

23.16 send-task-failure

A worker invokes send-task-failure to report that the task identified by the taskToken failed.

23.17 send-task-heartbeat

A worker invokes send-task-heartbeat to report that a long-lived task identified by the taskToken is still making progress. This action resets the Heartbeat clock.

24 Step Function SDKs

AWS SDKs provide a set of language-specific function calls for Step Functions.

24.1 Node.js

The AWS SDK for Node.js is installed using the npm package manager. To install, type the following into a terminal window:

```
npm install aws-sdk
```

Import `aws-sdk` in a JavaScript file as follows:

```
// import entire SDK
var AWS = require('aws-sdk');
// import AWS object without services
var AWS = require('aws-sdk/global');
// import individual service
var S3 = require('aws-sdk/clients/s3');
```

24.2 Python

The AWS SDK for Python is Boto3. There is a low-level client that represents AWS Step Functions. This is imported in a Python file as follows:

```
import boto3
sfn_client = boto3.client('stepfunctions')
```

The Python APIs for Step Function (SFN) client are shown below.

- can_paginate()
- create_activity()
- create_state_machine()
- delete_activity()
- delete_state_machine()
- describe_activity()
- describe_execution()
- describe_state_machine()
- generate_presigned_url()
- get_activity_task()
- get_execution_history()
- get_paginator()
- get_waiter()
- list_activities()
- list_executions()
- list_state_machines()
- send_task_failure()
- send_task_heartbeat()

- send_task_success()
- start_execution()
- stop_execution()

A state machine may be created as shown below.

```
response = sfn_client.create_state_machine(
    name=step-function-name,
    definition=state-machine-asl-definition,
    roleArn=role-arn
)


response = client.invoke(
    FunctionName='string',
    InvocationType='Event'|'RequestResponse'|'DryRun',
    LogType='None'|'Tail',
    ClientContext='string',
    Payload=b'bytes'|file,
    Qualifier='string'
)
```

24.2.1 Paginators

The Boto3 package provides a paginator API that can be used in cases where an incomplete result is returned on an initial request and repeated requests are required to get the complete results. A subsequent response continues from the point the previous response left off. Available paginators include:

- SFN.Paginator.GetExecutionHistory
- SFN.Paginator.ListActivities
- SFN.Paginator.ListExecutions
- SFN.Paginator.ListStateMachines

For example, the GetExecutionHistory paginator can be used are follows:

```
response_iterator = paginator.paginate(
    executionArn='string',
    reverseOrder=True|False,
    PaginationConfig={
        'MaxItems': 123,
        'PageSize': 123,
        'StartingToken': 'string'
    }
)
```

25 Validation, Limits and Pricing

25.1 StateLint

StateLint is a Ruby Gem that provides a command-line validator for Amazon States Language JSON files. StateLint performs syntax and semantic validation on the state machine language definition and displays error messages if any violations are encountered. It is invoked from the CLI with the ASL specification files as parameters:

```
statelint <asl-spec>, <asl-spec> ...
```

StateLint is available at the AWSlabs GitHub repository:

```
https://github.com/awslabs/statelint
```

Download and install statelint as follows:

```
gem install statelint
Fetching: j2119-0.1.0.gem (100%)
Successfully installed j2119-0.1.0
Fetching: statelint-0.1.0.gem (100%)
Successfully installed statelint-0.1.0
Parsing documentation for j2119-0.1.0
Installing ri documentation for j2119-0.1.0
Parsing documentation for statelint-0.1.0
Installing ri documentation for statelint-0.1.0
Done installing documentation for j2119, statelint after 1
seconds
2 gems installed
```

Validate the State Language files using statelint. This example shows statelint detecting a missing brace.

```
statelint foo.sm-spec
One error:
 Problem reading/parsing JSON: 776: unexpected token at
'{
  "StartAt":"foo",
  "States":{
    "foo":{
      "Type":"Pass",
      "End":true
  }
}'
```

25.2 Limits

25.2.1 Lambda Function Limits

The following table lists the Lambda function runtime resource limits.

Resource Limits	Default Limit
Ephemeral disk capacity ("/tmp" space)	512 MB
Number of file descriptors	1,024
Number of processes and threads (combined total)	1,024
Maximum execution duration per request	300 seconds
Request body payload size (RequestResponse)	6 MB
Request body payload size (Event)	128 K
Response body payload size (RequestResponse)	6 MB
Dead Letter body payload size (Event)	128 K

The following table lists deployment limits.

Deployment Limits	Default Limit
Lambda function deployment package size (.zip/.jar file)	50 MB
Total size of all the deployment packages that can be uploaded per region	75 GB
Size of code/dependencies that you can zip into a deployment package (uncompressed zip/jar size)	250 MB
Total size of environment variables set	4 KB

25.2.2 Step Function Limits

The following table lists the general Step Function limits.

General Limits	Default Limit
Maximum number of state machines and activities	10000
API call limit	May be throttled
Maximum request size	1 MB per request

The following table lists Step Function execution limits.

Function Execution Limits	Default Limit
Maximum open executions	1000000
Maximum execution time	1 year
Maximum execution history size	25,000 events
Execution idle time limit	1 year
Execution history retention time limit	90 days

The following table lists task execution limits.

Task Execution Limits	Default Limit
Maximum task execution time	1 year
Maximum time task is kept in the queue	1 year
Maximum open activities	1,000 per execution
Maximum input/result data size	32,000 characters

Certain Step Functions API calls have throttling limits that use a token bucket scheme.

Throttling Limits	Bucket Size	Refill Rate
CreateActivity	100	1
CreateStateMachine	100	1
DeleteActivity	100	1
DeleteStateMachine	100	1
DescribeActivity	200	1
DescribeExecution	200	1
DescribeStateMachine	200	1
GetActivityTask	1000	10
GetStateMachine	500	1
List Activities	100	1
ListExecutions	100	1
ListStateMachines	100	1
SendTaskFailure	1000	10
SendTaskHeartbeat	1000	10
SendTaskSuccess	1000	10
StartExecution	100	2
StopExecution	100	2

25.3 Pricing Charges

Step Functions are charged based on the number of state transitions to complete the end-to-end execution of the state machine. Each state machine transition between states is charged, beginning with the transition from the start of the state machine to the first state, and completing with the transition from the final state to the end of the state machine.

- The initial free tier offers 4,000 free state transitions per month.

- Thereafter the charges are $0.025 per 1,000 state transitions.

All charges are metered daily and billed monthly. There are additional charges if the Step function uses other AWS services. For example, if the state machine invokes Lambda functions, there are charges for each request and for the duration of each Lambda function.

25.3.1 Pricing Examples

The state machine shown below has three state transitions, shown as arrows, through two states from the start to the end of the state machine. If an error retry occurs within a state, an additional state transition charge will be incurred.

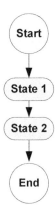

Figure 49: State Transition Pricing

The state machine shown below has four paths from the start to the end of the state machine. The paths taken through states 2 and 3 have four transitions from the start to the end. The path through state 4 has three transitions and the path through state 2 alone has two transitions. Error retries in any state will be charged for additional transitions.

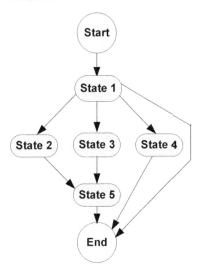

Figure 50: State Transition Pricing – Multiple Paths

26 Further Reading

26.1 Books

You will find these books very helpful.

Golden, Bernard. 2014. *Amazon Web Services for Dummies*, John Wiley & Sons, Inc.

Sbarski, P, Kroonenburg, S. 2017 *Serverless Architectures on AWS*, Manning

Poccia, D. 2017. *AWS Lambda in Action: Event-driven Serverless Applications*, Manning

Wittig, Andreas, Wittig, Michael 2016 *Amazon Web Services in Action*, Manning

26.2 Websites

Here is a list of web-sites that will help you learn more about AWS.

26.2.1 AWS Documentation

AWS Datasets
https://aws.amazon.com/datasets/

AWS Documentation
http://docs.aws.amazon.com/

AWSLabs
https://github.com/awslabs

Windows Powershell
https://aws.amazon.com/powershell/

Serverless Application Model (SAM)
https://github.com/awslabs/serverless-application-model

26.2.2 Lambda Functions

CLI
http://docs.aws.amazon.com/cli/latest/reference/lambda/

Go SDK
http://docs.aws.amazon.com/sdk-for-go/api/service/lambda/

Java SDK
http://docs.aws.amazon.com/AWSJavaSDK/latest/javadoc/index.html

Javascript SDK
http://docs.aws.amazon.com/AWSJavaScriptSDK/latest/AWS/Lambda.html

PHP SDK
http://docs.aws.amazon.com/aws-sdk-php/v3/api/api-lambda-2015-03-31.html

Python SDK
https://boto3.readthedocs.io/en/latest/reference/services/lambda.html

Ruby SDK
http://docs.aws.amazon.com/sdkforruby/api/Aws/Lambda.html

26.2.3 Step Functions

CLI
https://docs.aws.amazon.com/cli/latest/reference/stepfunctions/

Python SDK
https://boto3.readthedocs.io/en/latest/reference/services/stepfunctions.html

Java SDK
http://docs.aws.amazon.com/AWSJavaSDK/latest/javadoc/index.html

Javascript SDK
http://docs.aws.amazon.com/AWSJavaScriptSDK/latest/AWS/StepFunctions.html

PHP SDK
http://docs.aws.amazon.com/aws-sdk-php/v3/api/api-states-2016-11-23.html

Ruby SDK
https://aws.amazon.com/documentation/sdk-for-ruby/

Statelint
https://github.com/awslabs/statelint

26.2.4 Micellaneous

Python-Lambda
https://github.com/nficano/python-lambda

Node-Lambda
https://www.npmjs.com/package/node-lambda

JSON and YAML

http://www.json.org
https://sourceforge.net/projects/nppjsonviewer/
http://www.yaml.org

Swagger
http://swagger.io/
http://swaggerhub.com

27 Glossary

ARN – Amazon Resource Name

ASK – Alexa Skills Kit

ASL – Amazon States Language

AWS – Amazon Web services

AZ – Availability Zone

CFT – CloudFormation Template

CI/CD – Continuous Integration / Continuous Delivery

CLR – Common Language Runtime

CWE – CloudWatch Events

DDB – DynamoDB

DLQ – Dead Letter Queue

EBS – Elastic Block Service

EC2 – Elastic Compute Cloud

ECR – EC2 Container Registry

ECS – EC2 Container Service

EIP – Elastic IP address

ELB – Elastic Load Balancer

ENI – EC2 Elastic Network Interface

FaaS – Function as a Service

IAM – Identity and Access Management

IFTTT – If This Then That

IoT – Internet of Things

JVM – Java Virtual Machine

JWT – JSON Web Token

MFA – Multi-factor Authentication

POCO – Plain Old CLR Object

POJO – Plain Old Java Object

RDS – Relation DB service

S3 – Simple Storage Service

SAM – Serverless Application Model

SES – Simple Email Service

SDK – Software Development Kit

SFN – Step Function

SNS – Simple Notification Service

SQS – Simple Queuing Service

SWF – Simple Workflow Service

VPC – Virtual Private Cloud

WAF – Web Application Firewall

28 Index

Printed in Great Britain
by Amazon

19693260R00108